# Tracking Kindness
## A Memoir of Life's Teachings in Kindness

### Myrtle Heery, Ph.D.

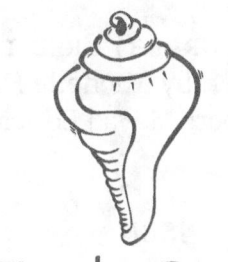

Tonglen Press

Copyright © 2025 by Myrtle Heery, Ph.D.

All rights reserved. No part of this book may be reproduced in any form or by any electrical or mechanical means, including information systems and retrieval systems, without written permission from the publisher. Scanning, uploading, and electronically distributing this book without the publisher's permission is prohibited.

For information about the content or permission to use, contact Myrtle Heery, Ph.D. at mheery@sonic.net.

COVER DESIGN AND INTERIOR LAYOUT
Bailey Olsen | Hank Designs, LLC
Typeset in Alda OT CEV and Acumin Pro Wide

PHOTOGRAPHY CREDITS
Back Cover: by Michelle Heery
p. 261 Epilogue: by Albert Maya | Education First Tours.

ISBN
Print 978-0-9894525-4-0
eBook 978-0-9894525-3-3

4940 Bodega Avenue
Petaluma, CA 95952
www.tonglenpress.com

*For my grandson Dalton and his generation
with the hope that they can learn from my experiences
and live with the priority of kindness
in all circumstances.*

*"My religion is kindness."*
—His Holiness the 14th Dalai Lama, Tenzin Gyatso

# Contents

Letter to My Grandson ........................................................... 1

Introduction ............................................................................. 3

1. Missed Step ........................................................................ 7

2. Sitting on the Steps of Inner Kindness ......................... 9

3. Grannie Wisdom ............................................................. 14

4. Dinner at the Ironing Board ......................................... 19

5. Happiness and Kindness ............................................... 22

6. Giving Money .................................................................. 25

7. Dede and Unexpected Kindness .................................. 28

8. The Houseboat ................................................................ 31

9. Returning Home ............................................................. 34

10. Waiting for Hugs .......................................................... 37

11. Watching During COVID-19 ....................................... 40

12. My People ...................................................................... 43

13. My Mentor ..................................................................... 46

14. Teaching With a Physical Touch ............................... 50

15. See You Tomorrow ....................................................... 54

16. Humpty Dumpty .......................................................... 59

17. Looking Over My Shoulder .................................................. 62

18. Elder Kindness .................................................................. 66

19. Unknown Kindness ........................................................... 69

20. White Privilege .................................................................. 72

21. Blessed .............................................................................. 76

22. The Truth ........................................................................... 78

23. A Kind Good-Bye ............................................................... 80

24. Waking Up ......................................................................... 83

25. If I Could, I Would ............................................................. 86

26. The Great Teacher ............................................................. 89

27. Forgetting and Remembering Kindness ........................... 92

28. Oh, the Water .................................................................... 95

29. Christopher Columbus ..................................................... 99

30. Creativity and Kindness .................................................. 101

31. Cooking ............................................................................ 105

32. Sacred Space ................................................................... 108

33. Picking Up the Bill ........................................................... 111

34. The Messenger ................................................................ 114

35. Kindness With Imaginary Friends ................................... 117

36. Four-Leggeds ................................................................... 120

37. Nothing to Do .................................................................. 124

38. Care for My Broken Bones .............................................. 127

39. Gift of Music .................................................................... 130

40. Good Trouble ................................................................... 133

41. Kindness in Kindergarten ................................................. 137

42. Surprise in Iran .............................................................. 140

43. High Tea ....................................................................... 144

44. Let Me Call You, Sweetheart ........................................... 146

45. Big Kindness ................................................................. 149

46. Caring for Property ........................................................ 151

47. Priorities ....................................................................... 154

48. Kindness for an Older Daddy .......................................... 157

49. It Is Not Your Fault ........................................................ 160

50. Challenging Kindness .................................................... 163

51. Who Owns This House? ................................................. 166

52. No Need to Fake Kindness ............................................. 169

53. Childhood Innocence ..................................................... 172

54. Secrets for Kindness ..................................................... 175

55. Kindness in Sports ........................................................ 178

56. Kindness Delivered to Jealousy ...................................... 181

57. Piled Higher and Deeper With Kindness .......................... 184

58. Luck .............................................................................. 188

59. Once Upon a Time ......................................................... 190

60. Magical Mistake ............................................................ 195

61. Dining With Kindness .................................................... 198

62. Gift of Kindness ............................................................ 201

63. Money Kindness ............................................................ 204

64. Kindness Meets Judgment ............................................. 207

65. Healers............................................................................210

66. In Gratitude to All My Caregivers ................................214

67. Somewhere Over the Rainbow ....................................216

68. Ground Transportation ................................................219

69. Imagination and Kindness .......................................... 222

70. On Her Tongue Is the Law of Kindness..................... 225

71. Self-Kindness...............................................................227

72. First Grade .................................................................230

73. Bumping Heads and Hearts ........................................233

74. The Quiet Student ......................................................236

75. Laughter .....................................................................239

76. Filling Mom's Heart With Kindness...........................242

77. Am I Next for the Ultimate Kindness .......................246

78. Impermanence and Kindness ..................................... 253

References..............................................................................258

Acknowledgements ................................................................260

Epilogue ..................................................................................261

## Letter to My Grandson

I do not know what world you will experience as an adult, but I do know the fundamental values you will carry throughout your life. When I was a child, Mr. Rogers would come on TV to help children experience life honestly. Here are his basic tenets for living a successful life.

"There are three ways to ultimate success.

The first way is to be kind.

The second way is to be kind.

The third way is to be kind."

— Fred Rogers

Being kind is not always easy, but remembering kindness is the key to being kind. It is easy to find fault with yourself, others, and situations. In those moments, remember that a life filled with kindness extended to all people is well-lived. At the end of your life, you will not be remembered for what you forgot to say or do but rather for what you did say and do with kindness.

You come from a long lineage of kindness, starting with your mother and father, who show you kindness daily. My hope for you is that you will remember the days of kindness with your parents in a home full of love. You will need this remembrance in difficult times because challenges will come in your life, as they should, to test your ability to embrace kindness in all situations, with all people, and within yourself.

A little Grammy wisdom: What matters is not what happens in your life but what you choose to do with it. Choose kindness, and your life will be full of joy and love.

# *Introduction*

Tracking kindness is often used in elementary schools to encourage kindness in children's emotional development. Children are encouraged to count how much they give and receive kindness daily. However, tracking can be more than counting. Tracking identifies animals by their footprints, which can take you into the heart of the animal you are tracking and change your perception of yourself and your relationship with the world around you (Vacha, 2019).

I recently watched a young girl running on a beach in Hawaii with the beautiful sunset glow shimmering in her hair. As she ran, I noticed she was tracking footsteps in the sand. That girl, happily playing and running on a beach, could have been me as a child. I experienced immense joy in nature during childhood, and it has always been part of me and inspired a mantra of kindness. Throughout my life, I have found myself tracking the footsteps of the kindness of my ancestors, family, friends, colleagues, teachers, and even strangers while simultaneously making my own choices and distinct footprints.

For nearly eight decades, I have found lessons in living through the stories of others and in telling stories of my own life. The stories included here span the 20th and 21st centuries. They begin in my hometown of Savannah, Georgia, and continue to my present home in Petaluma, California. They include where I lived and traveled: Afghanistan, Holland, Germany, India, Iran, Pakistan, Switzerland, and Turkey. I have experienced the sorrows and joys of living, all the paradoxes of becoming a human of 78 years. I am on this earth trying to make sense of being here. Furthermore, through it all, I have lived in amazement at the central theme of my life: tracking kindness.

I have written this book for anyone searching for meaning and ready to embrace and track kindness. I know not everyone is searching for meaning. Some are on a journey of accumulation, while others are simply surviving. However, those of you who have the luxury, privilege, or torture of wondering what "living" is all about may find something helpful in the following pages—a fresh acquaintance with kindness as the key to a meaningful life.

The search—not the achievement—is what I am sharing through my stories. After reading some of them, you may say,

"I could have written that." Of course, you could have; there are more stories of kindness than we know. I invite you to reflect on your stories of kindness. Your questions of meaning-making can turn into answers as we share our stories and build a future based on tracking kindness.

One of my stories of kindness happened in June 2022 when I missed a step and broke my right foot and left ankle. I had surgery, followed by a CAT scan to see if and how the surgery had helped. As I entered the CAT scan, I closed my eyes. Immediately, I saw a horrific image of dead bodies and could not make it go away. Everyone was clad in military fatigues. I saw many, many dead bodies. They looked like they were from WWII, but I knew they were from a new war. Many people were dead or wounded, and others were weeping as they walked through the carnage. Everyone was clad in army fatigues, not from any particular country, but definitely from the military. Then I heard a voice say, "Two-leggeds are stupid." "You are damn right they are!" I said to myself as the view of war's horrors continued. Then the voice said, "Kindness." Again, there was a pause. "Kindness ... Kindness to self and everyone always." "Kindness ... Kindness."

I was brought out of the CAT scan saying, "Kindness." The aide pulling my gurney said, "Yes, that is what we have and can use daily kindness." He shared that his arm was tattooed in memory of his friend shot to death by gang members, and still, he practices kindness.

The voice instructed me to show kindness to myself and others daily. It is not easy, but I am dedicated to this practice: acknowledging and tracking the kindness I have given or received each day.

I ask you, dear reader, to leave your judgments, good or bad, outside this book as you read along. Invite your curiosity as you read and engage with your tracking of kindness. Through these stories, kindness will take on new perspectives. I also hope this will open you to awareness and experiences that may help you connect with humanity and meaning in your life.

My dream is big, but why not dream big? My instruction has been kindness, and I am following my orders. I invite you to join me in this dream and begin tracking kindness in your life. Questions at the end of each chapter will hopefully engage you with your kindness.

# Missed Step

I made a human error and missed a step on a staircase in my home on June 6, 2022. I had been up and down these steps many times in 40 years. No, I was not rushing, no alcohol, and it was broad daylight; I missed a step. Most people do not want to hear this fact because it is too close to home—*Oh no! This could be me!* With all its frailties, the human condition binds and connects us, like it or not.

I broke my right foot and left ankle. I was alone, so I pulled myself on my belly down another flight of stairs and got to my cell phone. I called my 36-year-old son, who called 911. At the hospital, I got to know the orthopedic surgeon where the heart of kindness was waiting for me.

After a brief interview in my room, the surgeon, who had communicated with me by staring at my feet the whole time, moved toward the door and said, "You know you are lucky."

"Really?" I said. "How so?"

He said, "I am a realist, and you are not 20. If you were, you would have a long time to worry about your feet. You do not have that long to worry."

"That is a weird joke," I said.

He replied, "Yes, I like weird jokes. See you tomorrow."

I will tell you I did not "worry" about my feet but reflected on the use of this weird humor. Worry left, and curiosity came tumbling into my brain. He was right: I did not have many years left at age 75 and was certainly not a sports star. That fact softened my anxiety about whether I would walk again. Several professionals, including the doctor, told me I would. My limited time on this earth allowed me to relax into the healing and care of my feet at that moment.

We all have ideas of kindness, but I invite you to drop your ideas and continue reading with curiosity. Kindness does rise its head and shower grace on each of us in many situations.

*When has weird/unexpected humor caused you to see a situation from a new perspective?*

*Has a physical injury ever caused you to reflect on the importance of kindness?*

# *Sitting on the Steps of Inner Kindness*

When was the last time you slowed down and sat on some steps? I will bet not recently. Perhaps you are exhausted from the daily input of information. After falling down stairs, I slowly began to get the choice of sitting on the steps of kindness.

I took many minutes in my rehab in silence and imagined myself sitting on steps. I am referring to steps that are deeply alive inside of me. As we all know so well, we are more than our physical form, more than the circumstances we are all living in at this moment, and more than anything that might happen to us.

This is t*he first inner step* of kindness. Awareness that I am more than my physical body. Yes, this awareness is a theme I know and experience daily. I sit with awareness, with my perception of who I truly am, and the circumstances around me become much larger. I take in the fact that I am larger than I can imagine. I also draw from my past experiences that reinforce this awareness. Whenever an idea becomes a reality to me, I draw on kindness that comes to help and assist me.

Many of us have sat as children at the feet of a grandparent. For myself, my experience of my southern grandmother was amazing. I remember, like yesterday, sitting at her feet watching her crochet on the screen porch of our rented old summer home at the beach. I treasured these times because I got love and wisdom from Grannie. Her hands had large veins, which I could see. I asked, "Why can I see your veins and not mine?" "You will, child, and when you do, you will know you are old and hopefully wise."

*The second step* leading into my inner kindness could easily be titled "let go and give back." In aging, I am amazed by how much energy in my life has been focused on survival and earning money, with the assumption that money and happiness are linked. Moreover, sometimes, money and happiness are linked. Most of my stories highlight what goes around and comes around. Being kind is a great payment for living a happy life. What has made me very happy is sharing, giving back, not taking, hoarding, or worrying about survival. As I sit on this second stair, I take a moment of silence to commit to giving back in my way by the end of this day and starting again tomorrow, letting go and giving back.

I now move to *the third inner step* and sit on this step. I take a deep breath and let out my exhale with a big Smile! *Smiling and laughing* are the third step. I get closer to inner kindness with this amazing miracle—Smiling and laughing! Yes, it is a miracle to smile and let go of a hearty laugh, so hard that my body gives into joy and my head throws back with relief from suffering, rejoicing in the mystery of being. Humor helps me cope with a lot of uncertainties and challenges that I face, no matter where I am. There is nothing more universal than a smile. I try it when I am getting hassled by anything in my life—Smile. Spiritual leader Thich Nhat Hanh encouraged those who are meditating to keep a gentle, small smile on their mouth. I try it as I watch all the thoughts my mind produces, and I gently gravitate toward the kindness inside.

Laughing in the face of adversity goes hand in hand with my smile. Often overlooked, being kind to yourself is the ultimate kindness. As I sit on the steps, smiling and laughing, I embrace humility by being kind to myself and others. If I am laughing, I am not experiencing adversity toward myself or others but embracing loving kindness and humility toward the miracle of life. As the poet Mary Oliver suggests, "Stay young, always, in the theater of your mind."

*The fourth step* of inner kindness is accompanied by *mercy*. There is no justice, but there is mercy, a reality a dear friend teaching at the University of Jerusalem shared with me. She never knew if she would return home from teaching each day, as there were random killings daily at the university. She had come to live the experience of *no justice but mercy* and, with humility, embraced kindness.

The four steps of kindness are as follows: I am more than my body, let go and give back, smile and laugh, and there is no justice but there is mercy. While sitting on each step of kindness, I reflect on what brings and gives kindness in my life. I notice what comes up and commit to paying more attention to these kindnesses. I then remember what gives someone else the experience of kindness and do something to help that kindness come into their life. It could be as simple as my smile or hug. The gestures of kindness continue forward, but the commitment to bring it forward is an individual responsibility.

I let myself be called to reach out to others with loving kindness. This is my individual and collective work. I am grateful I have arrived at my inner steps of kindness.

I am committed to sitting on these inner steps daily—in silence—so I can be a clear messenger of kindness from the inside out. And in Mary Oliver's words:

Bless the words with which I try to say

what I see, think, or feel.

With gratitude for the grace of the earth.

The expected and the exception, both.

For all the hours I have been given to

Be in this world

(Oliver, 2016)

*Can you choose a step or two of kindness...to sit upon and dive deep into its gift?*

*Can you make a one-day commitment to be kind to yourself?*

# *Grannie Wisdom*

I remember sitting at the feet of my grandmother, watching her fingers move quickly, pulling fine threads through two needles, creating to my eyes the most beautiful table mat I had ever seen. She was crocheting. I was five years old. We sat on the big screened porch of our summer home at Savannah Beach, known to the locals as "Tybee." An average day's temperature and humidity of 90 degrees would bring our afternoons to a screeching stop. We used fans to cool off and swatted mosquitos with tightly rolled-up papers. Boredom was part of the hot afternoons. Some would read, and others would sleep. Nevertheless, those were the hours I chose to watch Grannie crochet.

My Grannie was tiny, maybe five feet tall, with piercing blue eyes that seemed from my perspective to see right into my soul. In other words, no lies to Grannie! She crocheted a lot. I would sit at her feet and stare at her fingers, quickly moving the thin threads with a tiny needle in and out, forming the most beautiful placemats, hats, gloves, and even huge tablecloths. The thread was either pure white or light brown. Whether she chose one color over the other depended on who she was giving the item to and for what use. When she would drop a stitch and go back and pick it up, I would look closely at how she corrected it. She quickly picked the stitch up, moving her fingers and needle back to the dropped stitch.

Those blue eyes never strayed from the work of her fingers. The mistakes were quickly corrected with ease and sometimes while humming an old gospel hymn. She showed me how to be patient, how to correct mistakes, and how to let go. Sitting at her feet, watching her hands working, and rarely talking was the setting for the more-than-weekly lessons building the foundation of who I became. When she did speak, it was profound.

I looked forward to those hot afternoons. I had Grannie all to myself in the still heat. I loved this little old lady with the innocence of a child chasing a butterfly. I became fascinated by her fingers and hands. They were strong and quick. I looked closer at her hands, and I could see her veins under her thin skin. I looked down at my hands, and I could see nothing under the skin; it was all smooth. Why couldn't I see my veins like in Grannie's hands? There must be some explanation for this, and I knew Grannie would have the answer.

"Grannie, how come the skin in your hands is raised and not mine?" I asked.

"Child, those are veins. The good Lord shows those to us as we grow older, reminding us that our time here is limited."

"When will the Lord show veins on my hands?"

"In time, little one, in time. Do not worry yourself; it happens to everyone."

"What does it mean that time is limited, Grannie?"

"Now that is a big subject. I will answer when you are older. For now, remember to use your wonderful giggle no matter what happens. Promise me?"

"I promise, Grannie."

We never discussed the limited time. Instead, she would tell me regularly, "Remember to giggle because you will need it."

"Child, do not worry; you too will see the veins in your hand when you age." In one quick sentence, I awakened to aging—I would be aging when I could see the veins in my hands! How amazing! I see the veins now in my hands. I am 78, still not my grannie's age, but I am aging!

Perhaps, the veins showing themselves to me and the world are one of the first signals that life is not moving as smoothly as Grannie's hands moved the thread, that the rough spots of living are becoming visible. The thinness of my skin is becoming much more tangible. As I run my fingers over my visible veins, I feel the sadness of grandparents, parents, aunts, uncles, teachers, and many dear friends long gone, recognizing that I too am going.

I have no clue what my Grannie would say or do if she lived in these times when millions of people have died from a virus or become polarized in their political and social views and actions. She lived through the Spanish flu pandemic, World War I, the Great Depression, World War II, and the polio epidemic. These tragedies contributed immensely to who she became.

The power of Grannie's wisdom is balanced by the tragedies I and millions of others have lived through during COVID-19 and continue to live through political polarization. She was right: Laughing at times helps me tremendously right now. Not to diminish the immense losses, both physically and economically, but to assist in bringing hope into the moment and the future.

My hands are like a faithful old clock, reminding me daily that I am aging and becoming more vulnerable emotionally and physically. As I look over my shoulder at my life, I see it with older eyes—hopefully, wise eyes like my Grandmother's.

This experience was a great gift of kindness for me. At Grannie's feet, I recognized that I would age and die and that the process of aging was mysterious.

*Do you have a kindness story about a grandparent or older family member?*

*Do you have a story of kindness that woke you up to aging?*

# Dinner at the Ironing Board

As a child, I would start my dinner upstairs at the kitchen table with my mother, father, and older sister. I was innately curious and continuously asked many questions.

"How come the maid cannot eat with us?"

My mother quickly answered, "When you are older, I will tell you."

I would routinely pick up my plate and say, "Well, until I get the answer, I am going downstairs to eat with her." I would march down the stairs, dinner plate in hand, and sit beside the ironing board where Nennie was ironing.

"Nennie, how come you cannot eat dinner with us?"

"Child, I will tell you when you are older."

"What? That is the same answer my mom gave me. Well, I am not older and will bring my dinner downstairs and eat with you until I am older."

"Be careful you do not get in trouble!" Nennie gently

reminded me. She would then continue to hum some songs that I would ask her about. Sometimes, she would tell me the words, and we would sing together. Now that was fun! It was also fun to ask her how she ironed and made perfect crease lines on the shirts. Wow, what an art, ironing! Moreover, you could get burned if you were not careful. Life can burn you, too, so be careful.

"Be careful" seemed to be Nennie's message about everything. She never resented her ironing job or not eating dinner with us. Instead, I watched a young woman thrive by teaching me how to live with kindness. I never got in trouble for eating with Nennie, and my parents left me alone to enjoy her kindness.

Thirty years later, Nennie and I reconnected. I apologized to her on behalf of my family for the prejudice she must have received. She leaned forward and shared facts that I did not know.

"It is because of being in your home that I learned to read. I was surrounded by books. I read to you." She read the same nursery rhyme book to my then-infant son, and tears rolled down my cheeks.

"You probably do not know this fact: your father paid me, which allowed me to pay for my college. He wanted me to be educated," Nennie informed me.

Nennie married a soldier, left Savannah, and lived in many places, with Maryland as her final home. She achieved her master's degree in education and taught school. My father's kindness opened doors for her, and she opened my heart to my parents.

*Have you ever found kindness in reconnecting with an important person from your childhood?*

*Have you ever been surprised to hear a negative perception of a situation corrected with kind facts?*

# Happiness and Kindness

The happiest people in the world live in Bhutan, a very small country north of India, south of Tibet, and next to China. Why are they known for their happiness?

I read about this happy place and traveled with a tour group in March 2017. Upon arriving at the airport, we met our amazing Bhutan guide, who summarized why Bhutanese people are so happy and explained how we could experience this happiness during our visit.

First, Bhutanese people are taught from early childhood to be curious about life, especially each other. The concept of judgment is almost foreign to them. If we wanted to experience happiness as the Bhutanese did, we were invited by our guide to leave our judgment at the airport, where we could pick it back up when we returned home to the U.S. The guide understood that this judgment we learned and practiced in the U.S. had brought us financial security, higher education, and many other external rewards, but perhaps not internal happiness. We all agreed to his request and welcomed his reminders along our journey. It was more challenging than I had expected. How often my mind jumped to the judgment of self and others as we traveled through many challenges, including late arrivals, van troubles, and so many other opportunities to either judge or lean into curiosity.

The second reason for Bhutanese happiness, according to our guide, is that the families live together in the same home. The eldest live on the ground floor of the family home, and the youngest live at the top. This practice of living with each other gives physical and emotional support to the growing family. As we traveled, our guide took us to his home, and we witnessed first-hand the generations living under one roof. The kindness within his home with his different relatives was terrific. They were all curious about us and if we needed any food, drink, or use of a restroom on our visit. There were big smiles and lots of laughter. Our guide had lived briefly in California but missed the family connection of his home life and was so relieved to return to Bhutan and his home. He had many wonderful experiences in California, but the disconnection and isolation he experienced were always there. He felt sorry for Americans' need to physically separate from their families and not experience the support of extended family. I was amazed to hear and see the loving kindness that the extended families had for each other. The closest experience I ever had to living with extended family was my grandmother living with us in the summers at our beach house. These summers certainly stand out in my life as rich with love and support. Could this be possible today in fast-moving California?

Another dominant aspect of Bhutanese happiness is their readiness to give back. The Bhutanese share food, clothing, shelter, cars, time, ideas, laughter, money, jokes—just about anything—with friends, family, and strangers. They have little and easily let go of what they have. The capacity to readily let go is the measure of happiness. The Bhutanese like stuff as much as the rest of us. However, they have a natural propensity to give, not through guilt, but through experiences where giving creates abundance. When people are generous of heart, there is space for the experience of kindness.

*Have you ever found kindness by living with your extended family?*

*Have you ever tried to live without judgment?*

## Giving Money

Growing up, I learned about "tithing" to the church. We belonged to the Methodist church, and every Sunday, I got to seal the envelope with my Daddy's money inside. After church, we would go to the Methodist hospital and eat a Sunday buffet lunch in the cafeteria. The food was terrible, but my sister and I would never mention that truth! Then, upstairs to the hospital, we would go with my parents to greet the staff and any patient who needed a hello from my dad, who was chairman of the board of this non-profit hospital. At the time, it seemed boring; no other family was doing this, and all I remember was being told I would understand this experience when I was older.

Sure enough, in my early twenties, this experience of giving to those in need became crystal clear. I was living on the houseboat, and my dear friends, whose boat was next to us, were pregnant with their first child. The morning the wife went into labor, the husband came over and asked to borrow $250 to get his wife into the hospital. I was shocked he had not financially planned for this day, but his family was barely making it with his profession as a designer of glass art. I was financially reliable with my uptown ad assistant job in the city. I wrote the check to him with the caveat that he was to never pay me back. This agreement was hard for him to accept, but he did. The precious baby boy was born and grew up with the love of his family. I finally felt what we had been doing in the halls of the hospital when I was little; to give to those in need without any expectation of a return was a total experience of kindness for everyone.

After I left the houseboat, I moved further north in California. About ten years later, my friend and his son contacted me and asked if they could come visit me. Of course, I wanted to see this young man! They arrived carrying a large parcel covered in strong wrapping. I went outside to greet them, and the young man said, "We wanted to thank you for helping me come into this world. Please open." I was so moved by his words that I could not imagine what they had brought. Carefully, I began taking the wrapping off the package that the father and son held. Then, there were glimpses of the content. A large, multi-colored glass window began to emerge.

"What is it?" I naively asked.

"The faceless Zen Archer, waiting quietly with bow and arrow on his lap to shoot when needed at the right moment."

"Faceless? Why faceless?"

"He is completely open without features. The openness is what you had when you gave me the check ten years ago for the birth of my son."

"Oh my, this window is gorgeous. Did you make it?"

"Of course, for you."

I was speechless. I had no idea the monetary value of this window, but it was surely far beyond my $250 check. The emotional value was huge. I accepted the gift with much gratitude and awe of what a small gift of money can bring.

My family then designed and built a house around this window. Everyone who comes into the home is told this story and experiences giving money without expectations.

*Have you ever given money without expectation of any return?*

*What monetary gift of kindness could you give a friend?*

# Dede and Unexpected Kindness

In the late 1970s, my husband and I lived in Turkey to earn much-needed money for our long drive to India from Amsterdam. My husband worked for a university on the American military base to help finance our trip. We were traveling with our wonderful Irish Setter, Tasha, which made it challenging to find a place to live, but we did. We rented a room in a home in a small village across from the American military base.

The home had a Turkish family: a mother, father, several children, and Dede, a grandfather in Turkish. It was next door to a mosque, and prayer was called seven times a day. Dede would prostrate himself on the floor in an open garden space in the middle of the home. I watched him daily with awe and curiosity. What was he doing? What was he saying? He looked so at peace with life.

I wanted to know what these prayers were, but I did not ask, as I am a woman, and it was culturally appropriate for me to remain quiet and covered. However, Dede knew I was watching him, and in time, he signaled to me with his hand to come close as he did his prayers. I nodded yes and stood nearby.. Then he turned to me with a twinkle in his eyes and signaled for me to stand next to him. He then showed me how to reach up and down with my arms to the ground, lay on the ground, and push back up. I never said anything as I did not know Turkish, and he did not know English. However, he knew I needed to experience the prayers, so I learned to put my head below my heart, reach to the heavens with my arms, and go down to the ground with my head and whole body to the floor. Humility is what I experienced! I did not need words. I needed to physically bow down in prayer.

Dede and I started having chai together after prayers. We sat in silence and sometimes smiled and laughed with each other. I learned a lot about communication without words. My heart felt so close to Dede. I felt like I was understood at the highest human level, the spirit level. To this day, I have no idea what the prayers were about on the cognitive level, and I am glad not to know. On the heart level, I know I became humbled through this daily prayer practice and often use the practice of saying nothing. The bowing is very similar to a yoga pose, but different for me with this experience from Dede and his faith in something larger than human. I feel blessed by Dede and his faith. I am forever grateful for his presence and his teaching me humility.

*How has someone given you kindness by teaching you a spiritual practice?*

*What unexpected kindness have you received?*

# The Houseboat

In the '60s, I lived on a houseboat in Sausalito, California. It was a year of adventure, for sure, but what stood out was the immense kindness that flowed down the boardwalk to the boats. People from all over the world, from all walks of life, lived boat to boat, not only accepting but curious about each other and all their differences.

Now, my daddy back in Georgia was also curious about his little girl, 22 years of age, living on a houseboat. He was convinced I had gone to California to take LSD. Those were the days of dropping acid in Haight with lots of publicity about these drugs, including free concerts in Golden Gate Park. Daddy provided me with tons of paper clippings of the dangers of LSD. I was not at all interested, as I had to maintain a job to pay for the houseboat, and there was no money coming from Georgia to support my living on a houseboat.

The boat I rented was at the end of the harbor and had a sweeping view of San Francisco Bay. My roommate and I got to view beautiful sunsets and go out on our "dingy" to enjoy the Bay.

Those were the days! I was completely safe, as the boat's owner, a San Francisco fireman, lived upstairs, and a couple who were both counselors at San Quentin prison lived in the front. Yes, there were hard drugs near our boat! One person with a heroin addiction on one boat whom all the neighbors kindly helped to get off his addiction. It was a very accepting community, and my Daddy in Georgia continued to worry.

Kindness became a mediator for my dad's worries when one of his closest friends came to San Francisco for an insurance conference. This longtime friend and his wife came to "see" me and my boat. I was very nervous. I put all the young adult mess away and cleaned fervently. Then I remembered the big challenge. This man weighed over 250 pounds, and the plank to my boat might not hold him. My landlord assured me there would be no problem and that he would be around the time of his arrival. He was completely right. He and his wife arrived and fell in love with the view and the serenity of the houseboats!

On his return home, he took my dad to lunch and said, "We missed the boat. Your daughter is on the right boat. I wish I had done the same, and if you see it, you will say the same thing."

Dad never got to see the houseboat, but he died (from lung cancer) knowing his little girl had made a good decision for herself. I had the honor to be with him in the hospital before he died, which I refer to as my awakening. His best friend came to visit one day and talked about the golf game they were scheduled to play the following Tuesday. Daddy said to his friend he would be with him, and he would do great on hole number nine. They looked lovingly at each other with moist eyes, a first for me to see with men.

When his friend left, I asked Daddy why he lied about playing golf next week. He said, "I did not lie, I will be with him, you will soon understand. My job now is to help those who love me to find their way when I die."

Daddy's funeral was the next Tuesday, and his friend came to me at the burial site and whispered, "Your dad was with me on hole number nine, the best I had ever done." We hugged for a long time, and, for the first time, I knew the death of the body did not mean the death of the spirit. My childhood innocence about death died, and I was awakened to the long journey of spiritual innocence.

*How has kindness helped you in your relationship with your family?*

*Have you experienced kindness in losing a loved one?*

# Returning Home

> Love is an ocean
>
> Without shores
>
> You have to learn to bear it
>
> You love your husband, father, friend,
>
> teacher, colleague
>
> And his love for each of us is a river
>
> That river is carrying us
>
> — Rumi (Barks, 1995)

There are few places I have been where I teared up as I entered the country. Granted, I was physically exhausted from driving from Amsterdam to India for months, but the welcome at the border opened my heart. The guard's large smile accompanied his words: "Please, have a seat; you have come home." He handed me a warm cup of tea with milk, which was necessary after my grueling VW bus experience.

The guard continued, "India is an ancient land with deep spiritual roots; you might have a feeling you are returning to your spiritual home." His knowing look opened my heart to his kindness and all the kindnesses we would receive in this blessed land of India. I now recognize we were part of a large group of people known as hippies, searching for the meaning of life through a pilgrimage to India. I do believe I experienced the meaning of life in my days in India through random acts of kindness. Everyone from the border to the south of India always asked if they could help us. Some beggars wanted our money, and, at times, we would share when kindness was sincerely present in the giving and receiving.

Of course, my husband and I did not agree on everything, and we would pass through tensions as well as kindnesses. I was driving the van down the main highway from Delhi to Bombay, which was cluttered with cows, which are all sacred in India. You do not hit a cow, nor do you blow your horn at a cow, but instead, you must wait as the cow gets to the other side of the highway, then proceed. My husband was convinced I had made a mistake and taken the wrong road, as it looked pretty sketchy. I was sure I was on the right road, but if he had a better idea, I would gladly follow it. There was an intersection of a small road, and he instructed me to turn right, which I did. This road was even more sketchy, but onward we went. Then, there were cows on the road and humans walking aimlessly. Where were we going? Onward we went as my husband continued to be certain we were going to find the correct highway soon. Instead, we came upon a large sign in English, "Indian Mental Hospital!" Was this for real? Sure enough, it was a real mental hospital with patients walking in the street, which ended at the hospital!

My husband was a professor of psychology at that time, teaching on American military bases to university students in Turkey. His earnings paid for many of our expenses, for which I have deep gratitude. Seeing the Indian Mental Hospital at this moment in time had some humor. I asked my husband if he would like to get out and check to see if they needed any help. We laughed, and I carefully turned around, not wanting to hit a human or cow, and headed back to the highway, which was the only highway to our destination in Bombay, now named Mumbai.

*Has kindness ever come to you while traveling?*

*Have you given kindness while traveling?*

## Waiting for Hugs

My Daddy was a judge and walked with the presence of a judge, dignified. Some men would turn toward him, tip their hat, and say, "Good afternoon, Judge." He was respected in the small community of Savannah and, even more so, because he took the bus to and from work daily for many years. He was among the people who voted for him on the bus.

Waiting for someone you love as a child is full of so many positive feelings, including love and kindness. When I was about five, around five p.m., I would impatiently wait for my daddy to come home from work. I stared out my front bedroom window, looking down the tree-lined, clean street with very few cars waiting to see what I considered a very tall man with a hat walking from the bus stop.

At age five, I did not care that Daddy was a judge. In my world, he was walking home from the bus and coming home to hug me. Fortunately, my world as a child was small and full of kindness.

Is a hug from Daddy kindness? Yes, it is. It is love for sure, but the kindness is in his eyes as he lifted me in his arms and asked, "How was your day? Now, is your mom going to tell me the same thing you are telling me?"

"I hope so, Daddy, but I love you."

There was no getting away from it if I had been "bad." Mostly, I had been pretty good, except sometimes I was off in my imaginary world and did not communicate with Mom. How many times have I heard and experienced kindness as Daddy reminded me to answer my mom when she asked me where I was and what I was doing?

"Right, Dad. I promise I will." I tried to keep my end of the promise, but sometimes, my imaginary world would distract me from her calls. She will find me, I am certain. I am so busy talking to my imaginary friends.

As I write this, my heart opens wide to my parents. My mom was 41, and my dad was 51 when I was born in 1946. They deserve parent accolades for raising a child. Yes, of course, there were differences and challenges, but the consistent kindness throughout my childhood made it possible for me to be here to write in gratitude. Moreover, the hugs at the end of Daddy's workday became even more anticipatory as I grew and could leap into his arms on the front stairs, never missing a step!

Thank you, Mom and Dad, for loving me with so much kindness.

*Do you have a positive memory of your parents or an older family member being especially kind to you in your childhood?*

*Have you observed kindness in parenting?*

## *Watching During COVID-19*

Today, in the rose garden of an assisted living facility, there is an outdoor gathering for music, beer, and bratwurst. I watch from the second-floor window of my apartment as people arrive in wheelchairs and walkers, all masked to protect from COVID-19. A balding man pushes his wheelchair to a table under a nice canopy protected from the hot sun. He puts both hands on the table in front of him and looks around in anticipation. In the distance, a lovely, thin, gray-haired woman slowly walks through the rose garden on her walker to this table. He watches with more anticipation. It is as if they are teenagers with a blossoming crush on each other. She approaches the table from behind, and he turns with a gleam in his eyes. He reaches out from his wheelchair to guide her with one hand, but it is not necessary as she is steady with arrival and sitting next to him. He reaches out to gently place his hand on top of her hand. They hold hands gently. The look in their eyes is one of maturity. It is no longer a teenage crush but a mature adult's gratitude for being together in their later years. Live music is playing: "Mind Your Own Business." Should I? Aging with kindness is everyone's business.

More younger people have arrived hugging the older couple. Are they family or friends? I do not know. My heart is moved by the kindness of these people. Different generations. The balding man looks gently at the young man drinking his beer, and they smile knowingly at each other. What do these two men know about drinking beer? "Brown Eyed Girl" is playing now, and more kindness is flowing as this group moves the tables and chairs closer to the music. The younger generations are pushing the wheelchair and steadying the lovely older lady's walker. The band now plays "Route 66," more smiles are coming from every generation at this and other tables. What a privilege to watch all this joy and kindness between generations. COVID-19 is lurking, but everyone is vaccinated and masked with hopes that this event will not be where they get sick but a time to be remembered with kindness. The band closes with:

>Happy Trails to You Until We Meet Again
>Some trails are happy ones,
>Others are blue.

It's the way you ride the trail that counts,

Here's a happy one for you.

Happy trails to you,

Until we meet again.

Happy trails to you,

Keep smiling until then.

Who cares about the clouds when we're together?

Just sing a song and bring the sunny weather.

Happy trails to you,

Until we meet again.

— R. Rogers & D. Evans (1952)

*When have you witnessed inter-generational kindness?*

*What music brings you kindness?*

# My People

In my freshman year (1965) at a small girls' college, Queens, in North Carolina, I took Philosophy 101 to cover one of the four-year requirements. Little did I know what philosophy was, but I wanted to check off the requirements as soon as possible.

The first assignment by a PhD philosopher was to write a paper without any references on the meaning of life as I experienced it at the moment. I sat in a study room in the basement of my dorm. A table, chair, paper, and pencil were all the supplies I needed to find the meaning of life. I sat for hours writing nothing and thinking about my 17 years of living. My life seemed pretty uneventful and without much meaning at all. When I reflected on my life, I appreciated my family but seemed to have innately different questions about life than they did, such as my asking why the maid could not eat with us. Now, as I sat for hours in this basement room staring at the table, I began to wonder about the meaning of this table. Thus, my paper on the meaning of life began with the meaning of this table in front of me. I let my thoughts wander about who made the table and why they made it, and on and on my wonderings and writings went. Do I dare hand this paper of wonderings in? Why not? What have I got to lose? *Your grade, you idiot*, my critical voices answered. I decided to hand it in anyway.

A few days after I handed in my paper, the philosophy professor asked me to stay after class. I was a nervous wreck. I knew he was going to talk to me about my paper, but it was not going to be good news! However, I turned out to be very wrong.

I sat down in his office, and he looked me straight in the eyes and said, "You do not belong here. Your people are in California." What is he talking about?

He handed me my paper with an A+ written on the front. What?

"Would you like to know about California?"

"Sure."

"Many people in California question life similarly to how you do, and not as many people in the Southern states question life but accept it as it is. For you, wanting to know why the table exists, who made it, and if we need it are all questions more individuals in California would ask than in the South. You will find your people there. We shall talk more, but do your research on California."

I went from his office to the library and first looked up where California was, then read everything I could get my hands on about California, the present, and its history. I could easily see myself there one day. Not now, but one day. The professor and I talked many times that year about questioning life. He encouraged my questions, which had never happened before. I experienced the joy of asking and being encouraged to ask more. Now, I was getting a college education for sure. Six years later, I was living in San Francisco, surrounded by my people, and I felt deep gratitude for my philosophy professor's kindness.

*Have you ever been surprised by a grade you received in your education?*

*Have you had a teacher use kindness to teach you?*

# My Mentor

When I met my mentor, Jim Bugental, I promised not to read anything he had written for one year while he supervised my psychotherapy cases. On the road to becoming a licensed psychotherapist, psychotherapy cases are being supervised by a licensed clinician.

My experience with my mentor was unusual. He wanted to train someone to follow the subjective life of the client without the use of theory. I liked the idea of no reading very much and was full of curiosity about how Jim followed a client's subjective world.

Toward the end of the interview, he asked if I had any questions. I had been drawn to a photo of a man with a wonderful smile on the wall behind Jim. So, I went for what was "real" for me, which I quickly learned was of great value to him. "Who is the man in the picture?" I asked. He reached back to the photo, picked it up, and tears began to moisten his cheeks. "This is my best friend. He died recently." He looked up from the photo and looked into my eyes with a presence rich with the truth of what truly matters in being human—human relationships. I was experiencing authenticity in the moment. This is how he followed everyone's subjective world. He lived it fully with vulnerability and honesty.

For many decades, he taught me through tears, humor, storytelling, silence, intellectual discussions, disagreements, writings, walks, lunches, and any opportunity he could take to question, explore, and follow his insatiable curiosity about the subjective world with great kindness. Case consultation was not "about" the client but rather the lived moment of consultation.

Essential to my consultations was what happened inside of me when I brought the client into the discussion. For example, my mentor invited me to pace in his office when I shared that my client often paced during sessions. This client had been labeled schizophrenic for many years. As I paced in his office, I felt the isolation and fear of this label, and tears streamed down my face. Words were not needed. I returned to see this client with a much greater depth of presence to her emotional pain. This experience of walking in another's shoes happened in so many different forms with my mentor.

After group consultations, we would often go to lunch.

Jim liked a certain restaurant that employed a waitress he nicknamed "Giggle Box." She had an infectious laugh, and no matter how many struggles we had listened to that morning during our consultation, listening to Giggle Box was just as important to us. Balance was always important.

In his later years, he lost much of his memory, but he took the loss as an opportunity to fully live what he had valued so deeply all his life—the actual moment. His last years were spent mostly with his amazing wife, enjoying the beautiful blue heron in their backyard, softly petting his beloved dog, and sharing many other wonderful moments of love and joy.

I struck a deal with him toward the end of his life. If there was a life after death, he would send me a message that I could not mistake. About a week after he died, I was waiting in my office for a client when a framed picture suddenly fell off the wall and landed at my feet. It was a poster with the words "Individual Choice and Universal Responsibility." I found tears welling up in my eyes. I was not sure, but it seemed to be the promised message. Being a stubborn student, I had to get one more message. Later that day, there was a letter in my mailbox from a local mortuary with the following message: "You too will die one day! Today, you can purchase your cremation for 50 percent off." I knew this humorous and true message was his voice, and I called his wife to tell her the story and see what her thoughts were.

"Of course," she said. "That was him."

*Do you remember the kind teachings from a mentor?*

*What are your experiences of the presence of someone you lost?*

# Teaching With a Physical Touch

I never wanted to be taught, but I did want to teach. Around age four or five, I arranged a classroom in my playroom downstairs in our home. I had a small blackboard, chalk, eraser, chairs, a few random books, and a long ruler to use for discipline!

Next to the playroom was the heating room, where the main heater was for the house. Once, the man from the heating company came to fix the heater but returned upstairs to tell my mom the following.

"I will come back another time when your class is not in session. I know my work will disturb the class."

"What class?" my mother asked him.

"In the room next to the heating room. There are a lot of children's voices with a teacher. I am assuming there is a class meeting in the room."

"Oh, that is Myrtle pretending to teach a class. Come, I will show you."

She took him back downstairs and slowly opened the door to the playroom so he could see that no one was in the room but me. I moved from chair to chair, using different voices to answer the teacher, whom I was also pretending to be in front of the class.

"Amazing!" the heating man said in shock.

"As you can see, it is not an official classroom. I can assure you that Myrtle and her class will not be disturbed by your work, so please continue fixing the heater," my mother said with knowing, motherly confidence.

I was left to imagine classrooms as I configured them in the playroom. No one in my family stopped me or asked me about them. I just did what I wanted in my fictional classroom without any disturbance.

This playground became the foundation of my teaching at the college and graduate school level of psychology many years later. Through my role-playing with many students, I developed a deep empathy for my real-time students of psychology.

After a practice counseling role play with assigned students in college, one student came to me during a break very concerned. Her counseling partner, whom she had listened to for ten minutes of practice listening, had shared that she was very angry, and she was going to go home, get her gun, come back to school, and use the gun in the quad outside. The student, rightfully, was scared but did not want me to tell anyone what she had shared. I informed her I would have to, but I would not include her. I knew who her partner had been. Fortunately, she was in the classroom during the break, and I spoke with her.

"I shared earlier that there is free counseling at the school, and the head of the counseling department is in his office now. He is available to see you right now if you would like to go with me."

"Why me?"

"Because you are very special, and he only sees those who are very special. Would you like to go with me?" I extended my hand to her.

"Sure."

She took my hand, and we walked hand in hand to the counseling office. Fortunately, my colleague was available. I had not told him anything but nonverbally conveyed through wide eyes that this meeting was urgent.

I introduced them and returned to my class with full confidence that he would end this potential violence, which he did. We spoke later, and she had been off her medications for three months and needed help getting them refilled, which he did immediately. She had a session with him five days a week for several weeks until she was stabilized and continued with him for the rest of the school year.

The student thanked me many times for taking her to him. She was grateful, and I was too. I had broken a boundary by holding her hand to take her to the counselor, but I knew that the physical boundary had to be broken for a much larger good. Sometimes, kindness comes with a physical touch.

*Have you received kindness through a physical touch?*

*Have you ever given or received kindness in the form of providing necessary resources for another person?*

## *See You Tomorrow*

We did not know in the 1950s what a geek was, but for sure, my neighbor and I were geeks. He was short and fat, and I wore braces—only one other person wore braces in middle school. He was a year older, which seems a lot when you are young. Before he transferred to another school, we walked home together from the school bus in total silence, just the sound of the shuffle of our shoes along the sidewalk. He always carried a big briefcase. He studied a lot and was smart. I had a knapsack with a few books. I did minimal schoolwork. I thought school was boring.

Like clockwork, as we approached his home across from mine, his Cocker Spaniel dog would come out to greet him, jumping up and down with so much excitement. They would greet each other and, without looking at me, he would mumble, "See you tomorrow." I also looked down with my mouth tight so he could not see my braces and mumbled back, "Yeah, see you tomorrow." Then, as I approached my house, my Boston Terrier, Bubbles, would bark for me from the window with great excitement to see me. I would run up the stairs to get a doggy kiss, which was a relief after the social isolation of school. My mom would ask if I wanted to ask the neighbor kid over to play. Oh no, that was not possible at all. She tried but did not know what to do with our isolation. Often, she would say how nice it must be for me to walk home with him.

I do not know if it was nice. It was intimidation. He was smart and had a big briefcase to prove it. There was hope when he would say, "See you tomorrow," as if we could at least depend on walking together in pretty good silence.

You can guess a little about how this story played out over the years. My neighbor lost weight and grew into a very good-looking, intelligent guy who attended boarding school. I got my braces off and had a big smile to show off my straight teeth. I was never the brightest in the classroom, but I was certainly one of the funniest. I went from quiet to assertive with different ideas. I went to California, where I became a professor of psychology and psychotherapy. After teaching at various locations, including Oxford and Stanford, my neighbor ended up in New York as the chief curator of painting and sculpture at the Museum of Modern

Art, MoMA! This means I knew someone famous from my childhood. I felt proud to tell people I walked home from the school bus with the now curator of painting and sculpture at MoMA! We stayed in touch through random Christmas cards and a few New Year's Eve parties at his childhood home, where we all got drunk and sang "Auld Lang Syne," the words of which include "a cup of kindness."

In the 1990s, I accompanied my son's sixth-grade class to New York and D.C. I called MoMA and spoke with its secretary about the possibility of some sixth-grade boys meeting him there. She called back in minutes and said he would gladly take the boys through MoMA for 30 minutes at noon.

I, along with about six boys, arrived on time to be greeted by Kirk, who immediately said to the boys, "Myrtle has probably told you I am famous, and you should be polite, right?" They all nodded yes. They were relieved he got how uncomfortable they were. He then said, "Let us go to the other side of the building where they are doing some construction. We can find out what they are doing — much more interesting than art, right?" Everyone agreed, and I lagged, thinking, "What is he doing?"

Well, what he was doing was brilliant. He walked them to the construction site and talked about sports. He told them about his favorite sport, rugby, which none knew about, and he explained in great detail. The boys were thrilled, and thirty minutes were running up. He concluded to the boys by saying he would have to go back to his office and to promise him not to go in the other room and see the pictures of lilies he had brought back from the Louvre in Paris. One of the boys asked if he got the picture in a bathroom!

"No, but if you want to think that, it is ok with me. However, do not go look at the lilies, promise?"

They all promised not to look, and then he turned to me with such kindness and said, "See you tomorrow!"

I replied with a big smile, both of us looking straight into our eyes, "Yeah, see you tomorrow."

As he got on the elevator, he turned around, and we stared at each other, holding our past and present with big hearts. All the boys ran into the room where the lilies were and stood in awe at the beauty of the painting! They proceeded to spend two hours going through MoMA and loving it. Now, I knew what he had done. The boys had been deeply inspired by art by first meeting them where they were. What a teaching in living for the boys and me.

I never saw him again. He died from cancer some years later, and I attended his funeral at the MET in New York, where everyone sang "Auld Lang Syne" during the memorial.

A few years after his death, he was in a dream. He showed me how to swing out on a vine from a childhood tree in our neighborhood. I remember going over the street and him saying, "Hold on to the vine. I seemed to go over many faraway places, safely viewing the universe, as I held onto the vine from our childhood." I awoke from this amazing dream, knowing I had seen him today and been shown part of the universe from a childhood vine.

Lyrics of "Auld Lang Syne"

Should auld acquaintance be forgot

Moreover, never brought to mind?

Should auld acquaintance be forgot?

And days of Auld Lang Syne?

For Auld Lang Syne, my dear

For Auld Lang Syne

We'll take a cup of kindness yet

For days of Auld Lang Syne

— Robert Burns (1788)

*Have you experienced kindness from a childhood friendship that has stayed with you until today?*

*How do you bring kindness into your friendships today?*

## *Humpty Dumpty*

Humpty Dumpty sat on a wall,

Humpty Dumpty had a great fall.

All the king's horses and all the king's men

I couldn't put Humpty together again.

(Halliwell-Phillipps, 1886)

Mother Nature gave the world COVID-19 and put us in timeout through required social distancing. Isolation and loneliness were rampant. As a result, many Humpty Dumpty's fell off walls, with no King's Horses or men available to put them back together.

We saw countless physical and financial deaths. The world was in an existential crisis. There was no need to turn to a king anywhere but rather to ourselves to search closely for the behaviors that impact the lives of others. By wearing a mask, we could protect someone from possible death.

It is fantastic to know that we can do this! Our conscious caring can put the broken Humpty Dumpty back together.

Many years ago, in my psychotherapy practice, I saw a mother whose child had been murdered. What can any therapist say or do in such a tragedy? I gave her my heart full of care, compassion, kindness, and love. Yes, I say "love" in psychotherapy. The love I had for this woman's suffering infused her with hope. Once, she asked me:

"Do you have a child?"

"Yes, I do."

"I could feel you did by the way you look at me with, what shall I say, love?"

"Yes, it is love."

"I hope this never happens to you."

"If it does, I will come see you."

Tears moved slowly down our cheeks as we gazed with love deep into each other's motherly eyes.

I will remember this mother and how much our loving, therapeutic relationship supported her in becoming more than she or I ever expected. She later started a non-profit for children from the inner city and organized many acts of service. Humpty Dumpty did get broken, but some parts were put back together through acts of service and kindness to others.

*Has had Humpty Dumpty ever fallen in your life?*

*Have you or someone you know had a loss and used kindness for healing?*

# Looking Over My Shoulder

As I look over my shoulder at my international teaching experiences, I see faces, stories, tears, laughter, and so much more weaving together. I am humbled by the depth of everyone's story and their willingness to reach deep inside themselves in front of strangers to make meaning of their lives.

I remember a tall, well-dressed Russian woman who attended a training I led in Russia. Her suit was the same and in perfect order. I noticed her physical appearance each day and wondered about her. I recall her certainty and quiet manner. I trusted she would speak in time, which she did, and there was the surprise.

On the second day of the training, I began speaking about the givens of being human. One given is death and how each of us carries the fact of our death. She raised her hand and said with certainty that she had cancer and might be dead in a few months. She continued to share that she was making the best of each moment, which included looking her best and being as honest as possible in all relationships. She felt grateful to her cancer for her present depth of appreciation in living each moment.

I shared through my translator how deeply moved I was by her honesty and courage. Since I do not speak Russian, I relied on my intuitive sense to connect with her and the participants at this vulnerable moment. I was sensitive to the depth of her sharing, looking closely into her eyes and gently moving my eyes to each participant. The caring from participants was palpable in the room. Some eyes were moistened, and all were moved.

I invited the participants to share their feelings with her if they felt moved to do so. One of the participants who knew her and her health crisis spoke with great depth of appreciation. First, she thanked her for her honesty with the group about her health. Then, with great emotion, she shared how her friend's cancer was an impetus to stop complaining about her life and begin appreciating it. By watching her friend face her cancer with dignity, she had gained a new life. Others followed with stories that were moving, and the group drew closer.

The experience of sharing a life-threatening illness with a group is powerful no matter what country or circumstance. In this teaching situation, the students immediately experienced the connection of sharing the possibility of an individual death. In teaching, there is a distinction I like to make between "talking about" a subject and the "lived experience" of a teaching. This experience took place many years ago, and I do not know if this participant lived or died. I do know that her vulnerability brought the group into an immediate depth of authenticity that I had seen in many other groups in many other locations. The fact of her possible death and how she chose to face her death was a huge piece of global authenticity. The possibility of her death brought us each into the reality of death. Even now, eight years later, I can still see her in my mind and hold this experience close to my being. The courage to share her confrontation with her death with me, whom she did not know, and with others who were mostly strangers to her, has been engraved on my heart.

Teaching in different countries can be enriched by being part of different students' and therapists' journeys in learning. When I complete a training session and wave goodbye to my colleagues at the airport, I turn to myself. I am surrounded by other travelers, but I sit alone. I look out the airplane window, remembering all the shared moments of courage, honesty, kindness, and vulnerability. I may or may not ever see these individuals again. There is a sharp aloneness to these moments, which I recognize.

I, along with everyone else, ultimately arrive in this world alone and leave alone. Life is with others, yet each of us is ultimately alone. This paradox of being *a part of* and *apart from* follows each of us no matter where we live.

*When has vulnerability (yours or someone else's) led to kindness and connection?*

*Is the subject of death part of your living?*

# *Elder Kindness*

In the 1990s, my dear friend Edith celebrated her ninetieth birthday. Friends and family gathered in her home by the bay in northern California to celebrate, remember, and receive. Edith was a granny to many, graciously sharing her wisdom with everyone.

"Edith, how does it feel to be 90?"

"Well, when I look in the mirror, I am always surprised and ask, 'Is that you, Edith?' The person inside feels familiar, but the person in the mirror keeps surprising me. You will have this experience, too, if you live long enough." Edith gently tipped her head back and gave a generous laugh. Yes, generous of heart for those of us who still recognize ourselves in the mirror and know that we are also seeing ourselves in Edith at this moment.

"If you live long enough." These words awaken me again and again. What about not recognizing myself in the mirror? Or perhaps not even being able to see myself in the mirror?

Moreover, if I live long enough, I will attend many memorials and funerals. I have lived long enough to look over the bay and remember Edith at her memorial. Edith died at age 99.

"And what advice do you have for us for living a long and healthy life?"

"Take a nap in the afternoon, not long, just fifteen or twenty minutes. Moreover, walk every day, every day. Start this discipline now while you are young."

"Anything else?"

"Oh, I am sure there is more, but these two disciplines are what has worked for me."

I remember Edith, with her veins peeking through the thin skin on her hands. A little Botox or face-lift might temporarily stop my face from aging, but I remember pictures on the cover of a tabloid (called "adult comic books" by some) at the checkout counter of our local grocery. The photos showed the hands of famous actors against their face-lifted visages. The hands spoke the truth, with all the veins proudly proclaiming their age. The faces spoke of wanting what had been and hoping for physical youth that was long gone.

As I live long enough, a facelift has dropped from my list of concerns. Life has a way of throwing us challenges in aging, which seem monumental and very unfair at times. I am laughing harder and crying deeper. Experiences arrive that scare me and paradoxically awaken me. It is startling to be told that I could have died falling down the stairs, but that message awakened me. Death is no longer the shadow following me through my life at a distance; it is standing right in front of me and staring me down. It can become the greatest gift of aging I have.

*What is your experience of living long enough to wake up to your aging?*

*How is kindness a part of your aging?*

# Unknown Kindness

After my father died, an older, distinguished gentleman approached me at the funeral parlor and introduced himself. "I knew your father long before he married, and we belonged to a brotherhood that meant a lot to us. He had a gold medallion from the organization, which I had come to get for the next brother. Could you please look in his drawers and see if you can find it? I will meet you here tomorrow afternoon, and you can give it to me if you do not mind."

"I would love to help you, but I have never opened any of my father's drawers and have no idea where such an item would be. Perhaps we should check with my mom."

He looked me in the eyes firmly. "You will find it; I know you will. There is no need to say anything to your mother. I will see you here tomorrow at 4 p.m."

Was he crazy with sadness over the death of my father? Who was this man? I knew I had this assignment and would do the best I could to find the gold medallion, whether he was crazy or real.

I made sure Mom was not in the bedroom when I searched for the medallion. I stood in front of Dad's bureau and focused on him, guiding me to this medallion. I spoke internally to Dad that I had no idea where this object was and to please guide my hands to it.

My hand immediately, with no hesitation, went to the middle, smallest drawer and opened it. I moved a few items back and reached to the bottom of the small drawer where there was a small case. I brought the case out, opened it, and found the gold medallion. I immediately took it to my room.

I met this unknown, distinguished man at the funeral parlor as scheduled. He waited with sunglasses on. He looked like the mafia. We exchanged greetings, and then I gave him the medallion in the box.

"Yes, I knew you would find it according to our instructions. You have delivered; thank you."

"It was amazingly easy. Who are we? Who owns this medallion?"

"We are a secret organization giving to others with compassion and kindness. That is all I can tell you. We work at the largest level to reach everyone. Thank you. The medallion helps in ways I cannot tell you."

We shook hands, and he moved past me to the parking lot. I never saw him again, nor did I ever understand what organization he represented. To this day, the source of this kindness remains unknown to me. I have speculated about this man and the organization, but I have left it as part of the mystery, which always puts a smile on my face and keeps my father near and dear fifty-five years later.

*Have you ever not known where the kindness you received was coming from?*

*How have you experienced the mystery of your life?*

# White Privilege

The wound is the place where the light enters you.

Rumi (Blake,1995)

I was born into a middle-class white family in Savannah, Georgia, in 1946. My father was a Judge of the Family Court. Anyone could call him at home, and they did. There were no cell phones, and the Judge's home number was in the phone book, making him an easy contact for everyone. People called regularly, and as soon as I could reach that phone I pleaded to answer it. Daddy did not want to take the court calls at home and agreed to have me appease the caller. He instructed me to tell whoever was calling that he would talk with them by phone tomorrow at his office. There was the caveat that if this was an emergency, they should hang up and call 911 for the police.

I was so excited to answer the phone using the most adult voice I could find in my seven-year-old body. I would say, "You need to call the police if you need help right this minute, and you can call my daddy at his office in the morning." I proudly gave them Daddy's office number and proceeded to limit the conversation and hang up the phone.

However, the people calling often wanted to talk, and I wanted to listen. Of course, the conversation would go longer. These phone experiences taught me a lot about people whom I would otherwise never have known. I was white and privileged in the South in the early 1950s. Most of the people who called were women who were being mistreated by their husbands, physically and/or financially. They were desperate and wanted the Judge to fix their situation instantly. I encouraged them to call the police immediately if they were in harm's way.

However, what was harm's way? I never saw Daddy hit my mom or even threaten to do so. Many of the women calling were frightened, knowing that the men in their lives might hurt them. I had my eyes opened to the dark side of life and saw the power of listening and referring those in need immediately to someone with more power than this seven-year-old girl had.

Often, I would run to Daddy after a call and report that I had done my best by listening carefully and then telling them to call the police. Daddy always seemed calm in his reactions to my stories, reassuring me that the police would handle the situation. I had listened to darkness but was also very protected from darkness. From these sheltered roots, I listened and learned that I was privileged—and with privilege came responsibility.

Many years later, I stood in a hospital for my husband's surgery to remove a tumor from his parotid gland. The surgery would take up to four hours, and I decided to bring my violin to play for the children in the oncology unit during these four hours. Now, I was a fledgling violinist. I was taking violin lessons with my son; neither of us was very good, but I often experienced the healing power of music. I took out my violin; a mother wheeled her son into the room. He was about eight and dying from cancer. I started playing my violin, and he remembered how much he loved playing the violin, so I quickly gave him my violin to play. His mother said she would go home to get his violin so we could play together. He continued playing my violin until she returned, and then we played together, enjoying the music with a growing group of kids with cancer listening. The mother was so grateful that I had come with my violin. She had forgotten how important her son's violin music was. What a profoundly moving four hours we all had. The young boy died several months after with his violin nearby, and my husband survived a metastatic cancer tumor in his parotid gland.

This memory reminds me of a wise saying: "The service we render others is the rent we pay for our room on earth." This hospital experience created deep gratitude for understanding the fact that we are simultaneously in the process of living and dying together.

*What experience of kindness have you had by listening to someone struggling?*

*How have you served another with kindness?*

# *Blessed*

I feel very blessed to have been in the presence of not one but two holy people: the Dalai Lama and Mother Teresa. What follows is my meeting Mother Teresa.

In 1982, I was part of the press corps representing the *Yoga Journal* at the International Transpersonal Conference in Bombay (Mumbai), India. I waited along with about 50 other reporters for Mother Teresa's entrance to the meeting. There was silence when the door opened, and a very petite woman dressed in white walked in and sat down with a large microphone in front of her. The room was silent. The room was full, and everyone was seated. I could not see Mother Teresa, but I could feel her presence in the room. The silence was palpable. No judgments and nothing but kindness permeated the room. What was there to ask? Nothing, so the silence continued.

Mother Teresa spoke simply and briefly. I only remember the summary of what she said, as it permeated my heart forever: Many people come from all over the world to Calcutta to try and help me feed the starving. I send many of them home to serve the starving and the needy in their hometown. You do not have to travel to find poverty and those in need. They are next to you. Look, and you will see. Then serve them with your heart, every day.

There was more of that wonderful silence. Then she stood and left with dignity; this small-framed woman with a huge heart fed those in need.

The Path To Peace

When I am hungry,

Give me someone that I can feed.

When I am thirsty,

Give me someone who needs a drink.

When I am cold,

Give me someone to keep warm.

Moreover, when I grieve, give me someone to console.

— Mother Teresa (1995)

*Who do you personally know who performs acts of kindness for those less fortunate than them?*

*Have you volunteered to help someone less fortunate as an act of kindness?*

# The Truth

At about age six in my hometown of Savannah, Georgia, I was in the kitchen helping "the help" shelling fresh green beans. I was standing on a stool, giggling and shelling. I had so much fun. I loved Vangie and would place my arm near her arm and say, "Look, I am darker than you, Vangie!" She joined me laughing and said, "You sure are missy, now keep shelling!"

On this hot summer day, my mother had invited her lady friends from church to have lunch on the porch. One lady used the restroom and passed by the kitchen to see me helping Vangie. When she returned to the porch, she said to my mother, "How nice of the help to bring her child to help her."

My mother left the porch to see what she was talking about and found me helping Vangie. I heard everything as I kept shelling. When she returned to the porch, she was horrified and said, "That is not the maid's child; that is Myrtle, my child!"

I quickly jumped from the stool, ran into my grandmother's

room, and shut the door behind me. Grannie was as always crocheting. "Grannie, would you promise to tell me the truth if I ask you something?"

"Of course, child, I always tell the truth."

"Do we have black blood inside us?"

"Now you promise me to never repeat my answer 'til after I am dead?"

"I promise."

"Of course, we all have black blood in us. Now go on about your business."

"Thanks, Grannie."

I was so excited! I knew I was part of Vangie, but now I had Grannie's wisdom to validate my knowledge! I continued shelling the peas, inching my arm closer to hers and smiling because my skin was darker than hers, and I had black blood inside me! I knew we were not different; now, I had the proof. What a relief!

*Have you had an experience where childhood innocence helped shed light on inequality?*

*Has kindness ever helped you with inequalities?*

# A Kind Good-Bye

Many years ago, my dentist was diagnosed with stage four stomach cancer. All of his family, friends, and patients were in shock. Moreover, the shock increased with the news that he asked us to attend.

He wanted to have his funeral before he died—to be there, to hear every word, to celebrate his life in the presence of those who loved him and whom he loved in return. His wife organized the event that took place in their modest living room with over two hundred friends, family, and patients gathered for a potluck lunch in celebration of his life.

At the celebration, he was in a wheelchair but completely mentally alert and highly verbal. His wife instructed us to share our stories, and we ate as the stories emerged. We all settled into the most amazing celebration of life because the life being celebrated was present! He participated, adding punch lines to simple stories. Moreover, there was a theme.

This dentist was very opposed to the Vietnam War; he organized and participated in many peaceful marches against the war. Often, during a dental visit, he would ask the patient if they were going to participate in the march that week. I rarely knew anything about the marches, so my answer was no, but I would consider it. He would jokingly turn on his drill to emphasize the importance of my march participation. It was a very common action he took with patients who did not keep up with information on the marches against the war. Many of us shared our individual stories of his drill and our participation in an upcoming march. The stories were both humorous and serious. He woke up many patients to the cost of war. Yes, he did use his profession to speak his truth about politics while you sat in his dental chair. Everyone respected him for this audacious act and his excellent dentistry skills.

He lived life to his drum beat and was loved for his individuality whether others agreed with his political stance or not. The love and kindness in the room were palpable. He was loved for having the courage to stand for what he believed. Now, he was attending his celebration of life. Another unique drum beat!

Observing and participating in his Celebration of Life has remained central to my life. Restoration of life came to him and everyone in that room that day. Returning to the home within ourselves, where we are full of loving kindness to ourselves and others, was at the core of this celebration. What were we truly celebrating? In part, it is to be kind to ourselves, despite any constriction, including how you celebrate your dying. Yes, celebrate and grieve the loss of life.

*Would you like to celebrate your dying before you die?*

*What forms of kindness emerge when a community comes together to celebrate life?*

# Waking Up

1966, I was honored to see and hear Martin Luther King, Jr. speak at the Johnson C. Smith University (JCSU) in Charlotte, North Carolina. I, along with my white college roommate, Leigh, were the only white people in the audience. Our connection to get into this event was a friend, Joanne, whose mother was a professor at JCSU. We had unbelievably good seats in the third row from the front.

There are moments in life when you know, even as they are happening, that your life will be forever changed. This was such a moment. Dr. King looked directly at Leigh and me and asked in his very strong, clear voice, "What are you doing with your life?" I thought to myself, "I am making good grades in college. Am I supposed to be doing something else?"

Again, he looked straight at us and asked, "What are you doing with your life?" He discussed the precious gift of life and the importance of using one's limited time well. Then I remembered what Grannie said when I was younger: "Life does not go on forever."

King talked openly about the fact that he would most likely be killed and said he was willing to die for his commitment to the integration of African American people. My thoughts went a lot deeper into his question. What *was* I doing with my life? This question became my mantra for many months after that event. I started looking at endings, not beginnings. College would be over soon. What was I going to do? A privileged life of traveling and drinking after college made no sense when I dared to contemplate my death. Meeting Dr. King woke me up. To sit in the presence of an awakened individual is not only an honor but also opens me to the importance of using time with intention and commitment.

Two years later, when I learned of Dr. King's death, I wept. I marched, sat in the back of public buses, wrote letters, and protested the injustices suffered by African American people in the South. I started living from the inside out, not from the outside in. I began following a much larger guidance from inside with a commitment to living with intention and commitment.

*Who inspires you to be kind to others?*

*Have you noticed any difference in your experiences of kindness when you live from the inside out versus the outside in?*

# If I Could, I Would

There have been times when kindness has opened doors to the core of my existence.

I met a child about a year before he died. He was barefoot and sat down to put on his shoes. I could not help but notice his beautiful feet and say, "My goodness, what beautiful feet you have." He looked into my eyes and said with certainty, "I would give them to you if I could." Behind the certainty was a calm knowing that shook me.

I gathered myself and said, "No, I did not mean for you to give them to me; I was just admiring them." Again, he responded with depth and clarity: "And I would give them to you if I could." I was truly rattled. I knew I was being taught from another plane of existence. We looked deep into each other's eyes and were transported to a quiet place of truth.

I never forgot this moment with this child. Excellent teaching was taking place. My soul responded with, "Yes!" He knew he was not of this body but of a much more significant world. He reminded me of this truth.

After he died, his parents became very active in organ donation, and many of their son's organs went to save others. I recalled the incident of his feet with his parents. We wept together, knowing fully that this child was a great teacher who came for a short time on this physical plane. Most of the community attended his funeral service. Stories like mine were told and retold. Yes, we had all been touched by a great being and had not known this fully until he left suddenly. What a gift for all of us and a great community drawing together through his loss. He left many gifts of truth with each of us.

I dreamed of their child. Another colleague with whom I shared his story dreamed of him. Spontaneously, I found poems and a large sign about eagles, his favorite bird. I found myself driving on the street where he lived one day. Not conscious that it was his street, I saw a woman being held while weeping in front of a home. A voice from deep within said, "My mom is being loved." I looked in my car's rearview mirror and recognized it was his mother. I knew this child was speaking to me. I rested in a space of awe and mystery of this soul's intention to remind and transform many people, including myself. What a gift to give your feet away and fly like an eagle high above the earth.

*Has kindness been part of your experience of losing someone?*

*Have you found yourself listening to someone who has died?*

# The Great Teacher

I had a police officer come to me for psychotherapy many years ago. He said once, "How would you like to go to work daily and be spit on by people you were trying to help and protect?"

What a question, sitting in a comfortable chair inside a comfortable office. At that moment, I let myself imagine such an experience, and I felt both rage and compassion toward the person who spit on the officer. When I imagined receiving the spit, I felt anger and outrage at the pain in the world.

Earlier in my career, I heard from a young girl in juvenile detention who told me the officer who had put her in detention had forced her to give him oral sex. Of course, I contacted my supervisor to initiate an investigation, and there were consequences issued to the officer, but, to this day, I am outraged by the pain and injustices given and received by so many people. A colleague, before dying from cancer, started a retreat center for men who had sexually abused others. He told me the stories he heard from these men were full of personal pain, which they then inflicted on others. These stories were easy to judge, but instead, he listened with curiosity and kindness. His listening transformed not only the men but also him. He had no judgment but deep forgiveness. I feel honored to have known my colleague and his transformative work.

In my career, I have been privileged to train many colleagues to serve others in emotional pain. In the training sessions, I have heard the emotional pain of my colleagues and those they serve. I have also had the great honor of listening to Veteran Administration therapists whose clients primarily served in Vietnam. They carried their clients' pain with great dignity and exhaustion. My listening to their exhaustion with kindness brought healing to the therapists. Furthermore, we opened our hearts to each other. Emotional pain is complex and unfair, but it is also a great teacher.

Many years ago, in a bathroom in Bern, Switzerland, an anonymous quote on the wall transformed my listening and experience of emotional and physical pain. I often share these words with those who share their pain.

Pain is the Great Teacher

Never flee from it

It bestows

Wisdom, courage, and eternal life

— Author Unknown

*Do you listen to others with curiosity and kindness?*

*Has pain been a teacher for you?*

# Forgetting and Remembering Kindness

During my life, kindness has not been my immediate go-to. Through the years, I have disliked or been disliked by someone. I have forgotten kindness and entered the game of dislike. Back and forth with the various dislike cards; who said what to whom, watching for nonverbal cues to play the next card of dislike. Dislike carries an inner price, energy. I slowly learned I did not want to spend my energy disliking people or situations. My "can you believe" stories lead nowhere. What if I met dislike with kindness? What if I expanded my understanding of kindness to include saying thank you and walking away? What if the person dislikes me or I dislike them, and it helps them or me to become more authentic through dislike? What if?

Rumi, a 13th-century poet, Hanafi faqih, Islamic scholar, and Sufi mystic, originally from Greater Khorasan in Greater Iran, said the following in his poem "The Guest House."

> This being human is a guest house.
> Every morning a new arrival…
> Be grateful for whoever comes,
> Because each has been sent
> As a guide from beyond.
> — Rumi (Barks, 1995)

Around November 2023, a new arrival came into my life. I connected over Zoom with a former student and a psychotherapist in Israel. She was leading bereavement groups and working with individuals traumatized by the continued war starting October 6. How could I help her? What can I do? Her answer was simple: support me through the grief and loss of those I am assisting.

"I can support you with a big heart of kindness. What are the loud noises in the background?"

"Oh, some bombs from afar, not to worry, we carry on," she said with confidence.

Yes, we do carry on as dislikes move into hatred, then dropping bombs that cause death, loss, and grief. Where is the kindness? Certainly not in the bombs that are destroying lives, but where? The kindness started in our long friendship as a teacher-student. There is a swelling of love and kindness from me for her and her horrific situation. Who is teaching whom? Of course, I remind her of self-care tools to manage her stress, but this continued war carries compassion and kindness burnout. This weekly Zoom support continues. She has set her limit for unkindness and will leave Israel to live without war and with kindness in 2025.

*Do you have a poem that helps you remember kindness?*

*How has setting limits helped you in being kind?*

# Oh, the Water

Water is essential for drinking, cooking, bathing, watering, nourishing our plants, splashing, swimming, etc. However, in 2025, due to global warming, there will be terrible scarcity and flooding. Floods destroy villages and towns. The drought and rising oceans make these times serious and scary for all of us. It becomes a paradox of too little and too much.

However, the hurricanes in southern Georgia were what was scary about the ocean in my childhood in the 1950s. Scary also meant exciting, except once.

It was about a week before a hurricane was supposed to arrive, and I was swimming in the Atlantic Ocean with my dear friend. We were having the time of our lives, giggling and splashing water on each other. We were not out that far, it seemed to us, but my mother started calling us from the beach to come in. So, we tried, but could not.

We were caught in an undertow, an underlying current, force, or tendency that is in opposition to what is apparent. The water looked normal, but if you put your legs straight down into the water, it would pull you down with a strong force into the ocean. You could drown if you kept putting your legs down in the water. We tried swimming toward shore, but it was useless; the force of the water pulled us further from shore. My mother swam out to be with us and immediately told us to float. "Do not try to swim or you will be pulled down under the water."

She also instructed us to scream for help when we had enough strength as we floated. We followed her instructions, but my friend quickly got scared and came to me, pulling me down under the water. I was terrified and screamed at her to swim to my mother, which she did.

However, we were all on our own as we floated and screamed "help" infrequently, as our energy to scream was scarce.

Fear of being consumed by the water was the dominant experience. I became determined to stay on top of the water, which I did. It seemed out of nowhere that an inner tube was thrown to me, and a lifeguard was shouting for me to grab it while swimming toward me. I did. As I held onto the inner tube, I kicked as instructed, which seemed very hard. I kept asking where my mother was, but the lifeguard assured me she was ok and told me to keep kicking.

My friend and I arrived separately on shore, each with our lifeguards and inner tubes we had been kicking with. The ocean looked so scary to me now as I looked out in search of my mom. Where was she? No one seemed to know. I was weeping and screaming, "Mommy, Mommy!"

Gently, a woman sat next to me and said, "Your mother is coming to shore. Look down the beach. She has been rescued by a man who was crippled from polio but went into the ocean and saved her despite his crippled legs."

"What? How can that be?" I said in amazement.

"Yes, your mother is fine," the kind woman said to me.

My mother ran to me, and her arms were around me, and we both wept. The crippled man tried to quietly walk away, but my mother would have nothing to do with his disappearance.

"I owe you my life! You must come to our home. Please, at least, give me your phone number."

"Truly, it was nothing. I heard your screams for help from my home and followed them to where you were. I could see you far out in the ocean, but no one believed me. I trusted my arms and legs to do the job to rescue you, and they did."

To this day, I hold this man's humility and kindness in saving my mother with deep respect.

*Did you experience a rescue story with kindness?*

*Have you ever reached out and helped someone in danger?*

# Christopher Columbus

After the six-hour surgery on my left ankle, the surgeon stood at the end of my bed and asked if I knew Christopher Columbus. I was shocked by the question. Internally, many curse words were arising inside me, but I answered without cursing.

"No, I do not know him, but remember studying about him in school."

"Well, we were at sea with him yesterday and have not landed. The seas were rough, had much turbulence, had unknown obstacles, and were full of mystery and unknowns."

What is he trying to tell me? Oh, I get it. "Are you saying that we might have to have another surgery?"

"Yes. I have to look at the pictures that were taken to verify if we have landed."

"There were no pictures taken," I said.

"You were asleep. They were taken."

"No, I would have known — check your records."

"I will."

The surgeon leaves, and within three minutes, a gurney is pushed into my room to take me to the CAT scan. I asked the driver, "When did you get instructions to take me for these photos?"

"About five minutes ago," he said.

"Thanks."

Back in the room, I did a little research online on Columbus and slept peacefully. The following day, the phone in the room rings, and the surgeon says, "We landed."

"Galapagos?"

"No, Americas."

Pause. "No, you are right — Galapagos."

"Does that mean we will not have another surgery?"

"Yes. Goodbye."

Relief and delightful laughter soar from my belly. We have landed safely with no more surgeries needed.

*Do you remember the use of metaphor for kindness in your life?*

*Have you ever turned to kindness in walking through a confusing dialogue?*

# Creativity and Kindness

I have learned much kindness in creativity, all kinds of creativity: sex, writing, photography, hiking, traveling, joking, cooking, and so many other forms of creativity have brought me many experiences of giving and receiving kindness. I am grateful for all these experiences.

Thank God for the birth control pill in the 1960s! My girlfriends and I were delighted to know we could have sex and not get pregnant. Of course, having sex was a secret, but staying up late and sharing with my girlfriends about sex was so much fun, full of laughter and fact-checking for not getting pregnant! The secret sex was what we called our sex lives. I explored orgasms with masturbation and with my boyfriend. There was much kindness in these early stages of exploring our bodies and tremendous respect because we were doing the forbidden but enjoying the forbidden.

Betty Friedan, author of *The Feminine Mystique*, came to

Queens College, and her words increased my passion beyond sex. I could become more than I had ever imagined. I did not need to get married and have babies. Instead, I considered living outside the structures that were constricting me. The structures did not permanently constrict me but rather opened me to new possibilities rich with kindness.

My creativity opened new horizons. I remember my first 35mm camera, bought in Germany from a military base by my dear brother-in-law, Wick. "You can do it, go for it!" Those were his words of kindness as I held a camera that had been my best friend for a long time. I photographed people of all ages, a variety of events, sunsets, sunrises, mountains, oceans, and myself, and created my dark room where I developed black and white film. One self-portrait was accepted in a photography exhibit judged by Imogene Cunningham. What a special moment in my life.

Who is Imogene Cunningham, you might ask? Google her name, and you will see she was a very independent, successful photographer in San Francisco in the 1970s. She stood tall in my small world of photography as she was a woman making very creative black and white photographs. She acknowledged one of my photographs—Wow! I continue to this day taking photographs, now in color with my iPhone, and I enjoy seeing beyond the human eye so much. Photography brings me a larger perspective on what is in front of me. Photography became one of my creative expressions.

On Fridays, while watching my grandson, I often make videos with my iPhone as he loves to watch himself on video over and over. At two, he loves to visit Grammy's home with the Buddhas. On Friday, he stopped by a small Buddha in front of my front door and informed me that my Buddha was thirsty. He immediately started pouring the water from his water bottle into the Buddha's mouth. I videoed this moment and could see over and over on video my grandson's immense kindness to the Buddha statue. Photography and video allow me to experience kindness over and over.

If I look at kindness repeatedly, I will want to look for more kindness. One kindness generates another, and I get to find the next one! I recently experienced kindness in a very creative act. I was standing in the grocery line for quite a while, I looked ahead to see what was holding up the line. It seemed the clerk was trying to get her supervisor to help her with an older gentleman with a walker whose credit card was not working and who had no cash. The young African American man with dreadlocks asked the clerk,

"Can I pay for his groceries?"

"Of course you can."

The young man slipped his card in, and the groceries were paid for. The gentleman thanked him and slowly left with his walker. I passed the woman in front of me and asked the young man, did he just pay for the man's groceries whom he did not know?

"Yes," he said, smiling, and I gave him five one-dollar bills.

"What goes around, comes around. Have a great day," he said, smiling at me.

*Have you experienced kindness in some form of creativity?*

*Have you been surprised by kindness?*

# Cooking

Cooking is not one of my virtues. I certainly have a few of my favorite dishes, including shrimp and grits! However, I know how to cook for my family and friends in crisis. There was a time when my husband and a close friend were recovering from illnesses and living in our home. Each required a radically different and particular diet.

My husband had been diagnosed with fourth-stage metastatic melanoma. My friend had developed acute liver failure while in northern India at a meditation retreat. She had been evacuated from her site and had spent a month in the hospital in New Delhi before flying home with her ex-husband, who had flown to India specially to bring her body back home.

Both my husband and friend were faced with life-threatening illnesses. Death anxiety was palpable in the house. However, instead of being overcome with dread, I used this moment of fearing death as a springboard to feed the sick.

I spent a lot of my time in the kitchen, mindfully chopping fresh veggies and boiling Chinese herbs. The smells coming out of the kitchen varied all day. These days were filled with cooking for one sick person and then another. It was far from preparing institutional food, rather, it was making certain that the diets were healthy and caring to keep all utensils and pots separate and clean. My memory of those days is one of learning cooking skills with curiosity and feeling moved that I could do something very specific that would help heal those I loved and cared for.

To this day, my friend remembers this time with great gratitude and awe that I could make different meals for the two recovering people with little to no resentment. Her memory triggered my memory of those days and how much joy I experienced during the healing of my husband and friend. Instead of asking what I could do to help, I offered to feed and house my friend and feed and care for my husband. All of this was happening while raising an active five-year-old! I do not want to paint a tension-free picture, but the laughter at ourselves and each other outweighed the tension. We were each long-time meditators and would regularly take our quiet time. The quiet carried us through these healing times.

*How has preparing food served the experience of kindness in your life?*

*Have you ever found kindness in silence?*

## Sacred Space

Home is a sacred space where support, agreement, and disagreement abound. The glue is love. Offering this space to another person is sacred. When the doors of our homes open, whether for a visit, dinner, or spending the night (or several nights), we are opening our hearts on a very deep level.

When my friends offered their cottage next to their home once a week when I worked in their area, I hesitated. I had to be convinced that this offer was genuine. Nothing was expected in return, of course, but to lovingly care for the space. It was not being used by anyone at night, and it would have been a delight for them to have me. I accepted and enjoyed the occasional late evening or early morning chats we would share about our lives and our opinions on multiple happenings worldwide. In addition, my friend began to leave fabulous lunches for me to take to work the next day and even dinners at times! I was profoundly appreciative but often did not express much gratitude, as I was tired from my long day of work and facing another long day of work in the morning. My unavailability for deeper friendship was a sidebar to their kindness that I deeply regret. Nevertheless, the kindness continued despite my neglect of our friendship. It is incredible how kindness keeps coming toward me no matter how little I extend myself back.

I witnessed my friends extend kindness with open hands and hearts many times to many people. Their hearts were open to others in need of anything. The same woman had worked for them for many years, and despite her aging slowing down her work, she came to make the morning coffee and talk about their families as she wiped down the kitchen counters. The love between my friends and this woman was palpable. I would often leave these lighthearted conversations with so much love that these amazing mornings propelled my work. I thank my friends for their incredible kindness to me and everyone they continue to touch.

I have stayed in many other homes while working in the Bay Area of California and Arizona, Canada, Colorado, and Russia; each home rich with kindness is embedded in my heart. Thank you, everyone; you know who you are very well.

*Have you ever experienced kindness in an invitation to stay at someone's house?*

*Have you ever regretted not meeting kindness with kindness?*

# Picking Up the Bill

Fighting over who owes what after a lovely lunch with a group of female friends was a shocking and disappointing experience in my life. I put an end to these experiences by paying for the lunch, which put an end to who owed what. I trust the old saying I have heard all my life and mentioned previously: "What goes around comes around!"

I have been fortunate, lucky, destined, or smart enough to not hold money tightly. At one point in my career, I traveled frequently to Arizona for teaching. I became close friends with a couple who insisted I stay with them, with all meals included. The only way I could "even up" their generosity was at restaurant dinners. I would excuse myself to the ladies' room toward the end of dinner. My mission would be to find the waiter and pay for the meal. My mission accomplished, I would return to the table delighted!

My friends were shocked at first, but, as future dinners

unfolded, the husband began to question my going to the ladies' room because he did not want me to pay for their meal. However, I remained focused, and all my missions to pick up the bill succeeded. I got so much joy from paying for their meals, and many occasions were full of laughter and joy.

The day before my father died, he sat up in this hospital bed with a huge check ledger and wrote his last electric bill. He closed the ledger, put the check in the envelope, and gave it to me, saying. "Mail this for me, please!" I did, and as the family moved through paying for his funeral, there was just enough in the checking account to cover the costs.

I grew up watching financial precision and being privy to my father's finances. He told me in high school that I would have to work, not stay at home with children. The world was changing, he said, and I had to learn about money. He opened the excellent bank ledger and explained to me what went in and what went out. This was my foundation of understanding money, its importance, and its powers. I saw who gave money to my father's political campaigns and his hand-written notes of gratitude. I saw how he picked up financially for others.

Picking up a bill for others expresses kindness, which might take years to be understood and seen. Paying for lunch or dinner is a drop in the bucket of life compared to paying for college. An open hand with money brings experiences of giving and receiving kindness.

*Have you ever paid for a friend's lunch or dinner?*

*What are your experiences around bills and kindness?*

# The Messenger

How could the topic of sex and betrayal bring kindness? I have such a story from my 1960s college days when going steady meant a commitment to one person. I was going steady and being very true to my boyfriend, to the point of not dating anyone at my school in North Carolina, even though his school was in New York.

A knock on my dorm door and there was my dear friend, the messenger.

"Myrtle, we need to talk." She closed the door behind her and sat on the end of my bed. She seemed focused on delivering a message.

"You cannot trust your boyfriend. He came onto me while he was in D.C. He invited me to come up to see him at his college when I saw him along with many others at a bar in D.C. Please trust me, I was shocked and, of course, said no. I could only think that if he asked me to go to his college and I was your friend, who else would he invite? I believe he is cheating on you, and it saddens me to tell you this truth."

I drew her close to me and gave her a big hug.

"I know this was hard for you to share, and I am grateful."

I confronted my steady boyfriend, who said my friend was making up the story. He said, "Maybe she wishes I had invited her."

"No, she does not want to be invited or go."

Betrayal involves lies that are very hard to digest. When a voice of kindness, such as my friend's, is outside the betrayal, the digestion of the lies is gentler. I chose to trust my friend's voice, not my steady boyfriend's, and began the long process— and I do mean long— of breaking up with someone I now define as a womanizer. I know how to identify a womanizer now, but it took a long time to grow out of my childhood innocence.

What was my takeaway? The kindness of my friend, whom I thanked again 30 years later as we drank wine in a winery in California. Each of us was married to different people with children. Again, I thanked her for being the messenger, as her message had changed the course of my life in a very positive direction.

*What memories of betrayal do you carry?*

*Have you found kindness inside betrayal?*

# Kindness With Imaginary Friends

Children often have imaginary friends whose families encourage or discourage them. These imaginary friends usually bring extraordinary kindness into the child's life. My stuffed rabbit, Chipper, was both my imaginary and real friend. Although he was a stuffed animal, I had a full-blown imaginary relationship with him. I talked to him in response to my questions.

"Chipper, how was your day?" I would ask him about returning from school.

"Pretty boring, just waiting on the bed for you to come home," Chipper sadly replied through my voice.

"Let me squeeze you tight, Chipper! I am so sorry I had to go to school. I missed you and thought about you a lot!" I would grab him and squeeze his almost rag of a body, holding him close with relief that I was with Chipper.

Chipper was part of a large group of stuffed animals on my

bed. I loved and cared for all of them, but Chipper was my first and favorite! In the afternoons after school, I think I learned to give and receive kindness, holding Chipper close to my heart.

When I was about nine, my mother and sister, two years older, declared that I was too old to have stuffed animals, so my mother, without telling me, gave all my stuffed animals to our maid and took her home to distribute them to children who did not have any stuffed animals. I arrived home with no stuffed animal and all his family. Where? I ran, crying, to find Mother. Where were Chipper and all my animals? She said I was too old for the stuffed animals and it was time to give them to those younger without stuffed animals.

"What? Where are they?" I screamed.

"They are with the children who live near Vangie. We must help them, I am sure.

You understand," my mother said matter-of-factly.

She had no clue what she was dealing with, nor my love for these stuffed animals and my imaginary life with them, especially Chipper. There were no words, just the word kindness. And now it was gone!

"Let's get in the car and see if we can at least get Chipper." Mother awoke to her error.

We went to Vangie's house on a dirt road with children

playing in the dirt. I had never seen this kind of street or neighborhood before. We went inside, and Mother asked if there was any way we could find Chipper, the old pink rabbit.

"Of course," Vangie said, calling outside for one of the kids to bring the old pink rabbit.

A small child came into Vangie's simple living room with big old Chipper. Looking at this child, I also understood how vital Chipper was to him. He reached out and gave me Chipper, saying, "Thanks for sharing!"

With tears in my eyes, I gently took Chipper back and said, "Thank you!"

And out of my mother's coat came a new stuffed animal for the little boy, not Chipper, but a sweet new stuffed animal. The little boy was thrilled, and I was too. To this day, I have no idea where my mother got this stuffed animal for the boy, but I do know that kindness returned in Chipper to sit proudly on my bed until I was an adult.

*Have you ever had an imaginary friend who brought you kindness?*

*How has a friend given you kindness?*

## Four-Leggeds

After being told in my CAT scan that two-legged were stupid, I was struck by the use of the word "two-legged. " In my experience, four-legged animals are intelligent, gentle, and kind. I have had five dogs and two cats during my many years. All have been amazing in their kindness to me in good times and times of struggle.

The first dog I knew was Bubbles. She was a Boston Terrier who was spoiled by our whole family. Bubbles was my main support during my later elementary and middle school years. She always greeted me with such excitement when I came home from school, and she was so eager to jump in my lap and lick my face for as long as I would receive her licks. I could talk to her for hours about my life and loneliness; she seemed to get me with those huge bug eyes. She even cocked her head with a little, "I know."

My second dog was a true mutt named Trollop. I got her during my twenties in San Francisco. She was half Border Collie, half

Shepherd, and so loyal. We spent many days running and playing catch in Golden Gate Park. She was so much like Bubbles. She even made the "I know" looks and wanted to lick me until I could not take any more tongue-washing. Trollop was my companion and protector when I drove across the country after living with my mom for a year after my dad's death. Trollop and I returned to the Bay Area after a challenging year helping my widowed mom.

The year and the drive back to California had one major event that stood out. I did the craziest thing and picked up two hitchhikers in Colorado, which Trollop did not like. They looked so pathetic and said they just needed a ride to the next town. Trollop was in the front seat with me, watching them carefully. She was very protective of me. When we approached the town, the hikers said they wanted to go further with me. Trollop turned around, showed her teeth, and growled at them. I pulled over, and they slipped out of the car quickly. They were the first and last hitchhikers I picked up. We drove into the Bay Area to live in a cabin in the woods of West Marin County, where Trollop continued to watch over me and bring me so much emotional support during those difficult years of solitude.

I went from a mutt to a full-breed Irish setter named Tasha. She is a beautiful and very smart dog. My husband and I drove her from Amsterdam to India in our Volkswagen van. She was a great help in making friends along the journey.

People were amazed we were traveling with a dog, much less a pure breed that was so smart and beautiful. We all slept in the van together at night and cuddled with so much doggy protection. No one ever bothered us because of her. Once, in Eastern Turkey, we were stopped at a cross street, and vandals came up to the van and started shaking it. Tasha immediately barked loudly and showed her teeth. The vandals were horrified and ran away. She got lots of praise for her protection then and many other times. This trip in the late 1970s could certainly not be done now and certainly not with a full-bred Irish setter!

And then, helping me raise my son was dog number three. Nazie was a full-breed Golden Retriever. I never once had to get up to a crying baby. Nazie knew when the baby would need milk before he even cried and would come nudge me. Once I had the baby, he would sleep until I put the baby down. He would remain on duty, watching the baby sleep until he needed food again. I was so grateful to Nazie. Thanks to him, I got some sleep in those days, and he did a lot more for our family over the 16 years he was with us. When he could no longer stand up after many acupuncture and medical treatments, we put him down with the help of our vet in our home. As he looked lovingly into our family's eyes, we knew he had served us well and hoped we had served him as well.

As an independent adult, my son got a dog as soon as possible, a chocolate lab pup named Maddie. When I went through my divorce, Maddie, my grand doggy, was my go-to with my grief and healing. We would lay on the living room floor together with her paws around me, reassuring me I would be just fine. Of course, she was right, but those days were hard, and her gentle manner took me through the darkness. Dogs can open our hearts with kindness!

There were also a couple of cats along my journey, Pookie and Gracie. Each had their timing down perfect for a lap cuddle and loud purr for support whenever needed. Of course, there were challenges when they slipped outside because there was a dangerous road in front of our property. Neither cat died on the road. Each lived a long, quiet life in our family home, giving out wise-eyed cat looks as we rushed through our days. They quietly soaked up some sun from the window, reminding me to slow down and enjoy the now.

*Where is the kindness in these stories of four-leggeds?*

*How has a four-legged brought kindness into your life?*

# *Nothing to Do*

Stirring a sauce or a soup is a delight, full of fragrance— the tasting and adding herbs are delights for the palate and nostrils. However, mixing the heart is a completely different matter. This stirring moves the soul, and I can count on it. Life can serve stirrings of the heart at likely and unlikely moments. I would like to share an unlikely moment with you, a time when I did not expect such a deep stirring.

This summer, I attended a new yoga class. I have practiced yoga for many years, but this particular class was a new one. It was taught by a young woman at least half my age. We stretched our bodies and stretched our bodies and stretched our bodies. I was feeling my age and was relieved to lie down. This lying-down yoga is called the Savasana pose, meaning awake sleep. What a paradox: awake sleep. How can one be awake and asleep at the same time? Well, anyone who has experienced Savasana will give you a big smile and say, Yes, it happens. On this particular occasion, I was deeply relaxed and almost asleep, but I heard this young teacher say, very adamantly, "You have nothing to do."

Well, my heart began stirring, and my mind said, What? I have nothing to do? Are you kidding? Nothing? And then the teacher said it again, firmly with such truth in her voice, "You have nothing to do." WOW! I have nothing to do, nothing to do. My heart started stirring, and if relief had a fragrance, this fragrance moved through my whole body. I do not know when I felt so much relief. It was as if my whole being was letting go of all the years of having something to do.

Nothing to do, what a revelation, nothing to do. I kept sinking deeper and deeper into a state of being with nothing to do. I was breathing, but the breath seemed to be just being, not doing. This doing was moving away, and being was moving forward—being without doing. WOW! Could I continue to do this when I stood up? By this time, the teacher was asking us to roll on our sides and gently come to a sitting position. The thought kept moving through me: "You have nothing to do."

I cannot tell you how relieved I continued to feel as I sat up, then stood up, walked out of the class, and continued with this experience of "Nothing to do." The being continued, but the doing kept moving back. My inner chatter kept slowing down, and my inner quiet kept moving forward. My heart remains stirred by:

"You have nothing to do."

I invite your heart to be stirred and "Have nothing to do."

*Have you ever found kindness in doing nothing?*

*Is it difficult to do nothing, and when you do nothing, you want to do more?*

# Care for My Broken Bones

I have been a patient in rehab once. First in critical care for 21 days and then assisted living for two months. Then, I went back to critical care for one month, which adds up to a total of three months of receiving care rich with kindness.

Until I was humbled falling down my stairs and breaking my right foot and left ankle, I did not really "get" what rehabilitation is about. The people who cared for me were utterly amazing, consistently giving, kind, and full of humor, which so often is the true healer.

One caregiver told me she knew I had not fallen down my stairs, I had fallen off my pole! According to her, I was a professional pole dancer at 75 in downtown San Francisco, and I could not wait to get back on the pole and strut my goods! In the meantime, she gave me one red spiked heel with a bottle of sparkling wine in the shoe! Plus, two miniature characters showing off their naked butts! I laughed so hard and kept the gifts in view in my room, so I always laughed every day.

My adult diapers were changed throughout the night, I was dressed and bathed, food was brought and taken away, and I was always asked how I was doing. The real question for me was how I could give back.

I got a friend to bring my Alexa to my room so I could have music and share it with my caregivers. I kept paper and a pencil by Alexa and asked each caregiver to write down their favorite music. Each did, and when they came to serve me, I would look at the list and ask Alexa to play their favorite music.

One evening, a group of caregivers came to my room wanting to dance to their favorite salsa music. They invited me to join by dancing with my shoulders since I was in a wheelchair. I had so much fun. They opened the door, and the music was enjoyed by everyone in the hall.

One time, a caregiver started singing his gospel song and shared that this was the song he sang as his young wife died from a heart attack.

I asked quickly, "Do you want me to stop the song?"

"Oh no, this is my favorite song, and it brings my wife back to me."

We listened in awe to his voice with very moist eyes. The caregivers were there to get me ready for bed, which they did, but they also got me ready for what it means to lose and move forward with a deep loss.

*Has music helped you in healing?*

*Have you experienced kindness from a caregiver?*

## Gift of Music

I grew up surrounded by music, primarily from my mother, who taught music before her marriage. When my mother married, she gave up her music career to not make my father appear as if he could not support our family. Those were the days when women stepped aside for their husbands to shine in every way. I know her stepping aside and leaving her music career played a big part in me becoming financially independent throughout my life and maintaining total commitment to my passions and my family. I did not give up my passion for my husband to shine.

Paradoxically, my parents met with my mother playing the piano at a party. Well into their marriage, my mother would play the piano for my dad almost every night. It was a love affair with music, but no money was taken for playing. Of course, my sister and I took piano lessons. Neither of us had the gift of music my mom had, but I developed a great appreciation for music.

Mother would get tickets to the New York Metropolitan Opera in Atlanta, and sometimes, I would go with her. It was a great treat to dress up and hear this music, which was magic to my ears.

Before their marriage, my mom was out to dinner with my dad at a hotel, and the waiter asked her if she would play the piano for a few minutes. There had been a request for piano music, but the pianist was not there that night. My mother had a reputation for playing the piano but would not play without my father's permission, which he gave.

She told me this story when I was older, with much pride and joy. After she finished playing for a few minutes, the gentleman who had requested the music came to my mom and Dad's table with his wife. He thanked my mom, stating they were from New York on their way to Florida and emphasizing how much the music meant to them. He then shared that he had not wanted to tell her who he was until she finished playing, which might make her nervous. He then introduced himself and his wife, Mr. and Mrs. Sergei Rachmaninoff! My mother said she could not believe what he was saying, but knew it was true when she looked up and the waiter said, "Yes!"

Many years later, in the hospital before she died, my mother looked at me and said, "Remember, I played for Rachmaninoff."

"Yes, I remember."

My mother gave up her music, putting her husband and two girls first, and great kindness came randomly to her in an opportunity to play for Rachmaninoff.

*Have you been rewarded in kindness after you gave up something or someone dear to you?*

*Have you ever been surprised by kindness?*

# Good Trouble

School was mostly boring to me, so I often watched the window cleaner wash the windows with such accuracy, sort of like Nennie ironing. One day, the window cleaner pulled me aside and said, "Missy, I see you overseeing me. I know you have window cleaning down, but I am here to inform you that window cleaning does not pay much. You better turn around and listen to your teacher."

Noted, but not followed, still bored. Finally, my boredom came to some good trouble in seventh grade in the Spanish class. We had a pop quiz, and, of course, I had not studied for it and made a 40 on the test. My best friend, who studied all the time, got 100 percent She was first called to the front of the class and given accolades for daily studying and 100 percent on the pop quiz. Then the teacher called me to the front of the class to shame me, saying I had made the lowest grade, 40, while my best friend had made the highest grade. What did I have to say to the class?

"Well, I did not study at all and got 40 percent correct, so your test must not have been that good."

Oops, he did not like that.

"Class, please continue to study today's lesson. Myrtle, you are coming with me to the principal's office." The teacher was very upset with me and on a mission to put me in my place, which was beginning to look like a pretty bad rabbit hole!

We said nothing on the way to the principal's office. The teacher requested that they call my father, the judge, to come to the school immediately. Of course, my daddy's secretary said she could not interrupt court for this request and to call my mom. They did, and out to school my Mother came. Sitting alone in the waiting room made me nervous. Yikes, my mother, this meant trouble!

I would come to find out I was in good trouble, the kind of good trouble John Lewis talked a lot about during his life. My mother had my back for a good reason.

We assembled in the principal's office with the principal, the teacher, my mother, and me. I said nothing. The principal politely greeted my mother, never looked or said anything to me, and asked the teacher to tell my mother what I had done in the classroom. He did, and then all eyes turned to my mother.

She spoke clearly and with great confidence. "You might remember I taught music and English at this school before I had my two girls but then retired to raise my girls. I have experience in making and giving tests for children of many ages. If I had given a test to my students and one had not studied at all, I would expect them to get a zero. Since Myrtle guessed 40 percent correct, as a teacher, there is something wrong with the test. As a parent, the fact that you, the teacher, tried to shame her in front of the class is wrong. I will be speaking with my husband this evening about removing both girls from this school. Moreover, never call my husband at work. He is a public servant. My work is raising our girls, and I am always available regarding our girls."

Mother stood up and grabbed my hand as we exited the principal's room together. Wow, she had my back! No words in the car. Finally, I muttered, "Thank you, Mom." Then she said, "You need to do your part and study every day no matter where you go to school."

"I will, Mom, I promise."

I stayed at the school after a little 'please come back and let's all move on' from the administration.

*Have you ever had a parent or family member stick up to authority for you?*

*Were you ever in "good trouble"?*

# Kindness in Kindergarten

I have had the honor of raising one son, who was exhilarating and challenging. At age 40, I was often the older parent at parent meetings. It seemed I often had a little more courage to challenge the boxes that education can sometimes try to put a child in.

I learned about the first education box in my son's kindergarten, where I volunteered to help once a week for part of the morning. Stations were often set up where volunteers helped the children with an assigned project. First, the kindergarten teacher and assistant instructed each volunteer on what to do with the children at the assigned station.

On this particular day, we were supposed to help each child draw a picture of the American flag. One of the students asked me if she could use different colors on the flag. Well, that felt pretty creative, so I said yes, and within minutes, the line of kindergarteners for my station doubled. The kids were creating multi-colored American flags, still using the shape of the traditional American flag. Kids were sharing and were so happy with their flags. I was also proud of them. Part of my job was to collect their flags when they were finished and bring all of the flags to the teacher's desk before I left. I collected their multi-colored flags and placed them on the teacher's desk.

As I reached the door to leave, I heard the teacher call my name, and the kids began to laugh. I returned to her desk, and the teacher scolded me in front of the class, with my son watching. She could not send these flags home to the parents because they did not represent the American flag. All of the flags would need to be redone.

I did not apologize but did say that if she wanted the flags redone, she would have to do it on her own time, as I needed to go, and I would not be returning for volunteer time the following week.

I was shocked and concerned about my son. I arrived early to pick up my son and chatted with three other kindergarten moms. I shared what had happened, and each mom was so kind and supportive of me. Their kindness grounded me. These three moms and I decided to get together for lunch. Out of this lunch grew our celebration of birthdays for almost 30 years.

My son and his friends thought the "flag incident" helped

them stand up to their teacher. They all loved their creative flags and insisted on taking them home. The children knew and followed their gut with the kindergarten teacher. I complained to the principal, who opened a drawer he kept for teacher complaints. Her file was full, and his hands were tied, as she was tenured. I filed another complaint for her, and I gained three long-term mom friends.

*What have your experiences of kindness been in education?*

*Has a negative experience brought out kindness toward you from others?*

## Surprise in Iran

In the late 1970s, my husband and I went on what is now known as the Hippie Trail. We bought a VW Bus in Amsterdam and fixed it up, making sleeping and cooking as comfortable as we could. The inside of the van was lined with wood to give it a wood cabin aesthetic. Only later to find out that, at some borders, these sidings had to come down in search of hidden drugs, never to be found. We were not on a drug trip but headed to an ashram meditation retreat outside of Bombay, India. Destination and process were two very different experiences.

Of course, on our way, the van broke down in Turkey. We were on a very tight budget, so stopping and teaching on U.S. military bases helped our finances for repairing the van and putting us back on our journey. Time seemed to take on a vastly different meaning without nine-to-five jobs. There was more time to experience the present, which was rich with surprises of kindness.

After driving into Tehran, Iran, with crazy traffic full of dozens of Mercedes, we treated ourselves to some food in the café of a very nice hotel. We started wondering aloud where we were going to sleep that night when our conversation was politely interrupted by two gentlemen at the booth behind us. They were from England and were so excited to hear the English language. We all joined at one booth and started sharing our lives. Within minutes, we knew where to spend several nights at their condo in downtown Tehran. They were in Tehran working as engineers, later to discover they were nuclear engineers. These were the days of the Shah, and much money was flowing into Iran, including Mercedes from Germany. Our heads were filled with politics, humor, family stories, and the thrill of connecting through the same language. We settled into their condo with access to a pool and a huge kitchen. I thought I had died and gone to heaven!

We were invited to an Iranian dinner in the condo complex, as everyone wanted to meet the Americans the Brits had found. I was told I could wear jeans but a long-sleeved shirt. Upon arriving, a woman in a burka escorted me to the room for ladies while the men went to a room for men.

All the women were dressed in burkas and were thrilled to

see me dressed in jeans. The minute the door shut, the women began to take off their burkas, and to my surprise, all had jeans on. Those were very, very nice jeans. Expensive shirts and fully made-up faces with beautiful hair. These women were beautiful and so easy to connect with. They had so many questions for me, but I had just as many for them. We laughed and cried together about life. Many had lost people or been separated from those they loved at a young age. My freedom to travel to India in a van was out of the question. Getting books and jeans were at the top of their desires. They were very well-read and fluent in English.

They wrote down the names of books and jeans they wanted me to send when I could. I was only given the address of one woman who worked at the University. They knew secrecy, survival, and sticking together. They loved and cared for each other in a way I had never seen before with women or men. I was surprised by their kindness to each other and me in simple gestures such as touching my jeans and a smile that went way beyond words. My heart was full of love from that evening until this day. I am grateful to them for allowing me to see their beautiful souls.

*When have you experienced kindness through a look or a touch?*

*Have you ever experienced kindness as a guest in a new country, town, or home?*

## *High Tea*

My dear friends have hosted a high tea in their amazing garden for our annual non-profit fundraiser for over 10 years. Many of their friends and I donated money to train minority students in mental health and assist minorities who needed mental health services.

These events were attended by 40 to 60 people who usually sat at tables with their group of friends. We had excellent weather except once. The first year after the hostess' mother died, the rain started at the beginning of the event, and everyone came inside the hostess' home where her mother had always wanted the high teas to be. As much furniture from outside as possible was brought inside, but the comfort of tables at a distance came to an end. Everyone sat very, very close, talking to others whom we did not know and laughing through this wet high tea. Somehow, the hot tea and food got served to all. It seemed her mom had orchestrated this indoor high tea perfectly. One participant shared that she had been to many teas in her 80-plus years, but this was by far the best. It required everyone to get to know and enjoy each other in very close quarters.

The high tea came to an end one year when the hostess came to me and said, "Everyone who is cooking, serving, and cleaning is 70 or older. I think it is time to stop the high teas." She was correct; we had maybe one or two people under 70 helping, but the magnitude of the work was too much for this age group. We are all aware of aging, which brings limitations in how fast you can move and what you can do. I expressed my deep gratitude to her, her spouse, extended family, and all those who had helped over the years, including one woman flying into the Bay Area from New York to make homemade scones! I am grateful to all who have worked hard for these memorable High Teas for many years!

*How has kindness come to you through others giving to you?*

*How has an unexpected change of plans brought you closer to others?*

# Let Me Call You, Sweetheart

When the ambulance pulled into the hospital driveway, there he was with my son. When I was lying in the hospital bed, wondering what was going to happen to my broken feet, there he was at the end of my bed. When the surgery went on for eight hours instead of four, he returned to the hospital to wait. When I woke up, he was there offering me some water with a straw and gently stroking my forehead.

"We will get through this together," he said quietly to me.

Who was this man, so kind and gentle to me? I met him on the Internet five years ago, and we had much fun together. However, this was not fun. I fell down the stairs in my home and broke both feet, and there he was, like a rock beside my bed. It was not *I* will get through this, but *we* will get through it together.

There are moments in life that are so precious and dear to our hearts that words cannot convey the intensity, yet I feel a responsibility to try to convey it.

He visited me every day at the hospital, rehabilitation center, and assisted living facility. We would drink wine together and laugh. We would watch sports and a little news and catch up about his adult children and grandchildren, as well as my son, daughter-in-law, and grandson. Then he would go home and call, "Did they get you in bed? I am just checking to make sure you are tucked in."

I am 78, and he is 86. He lost his wife to cancer, and I lost my husband in a divorce. I dated 40 men on the internet before I had coffee with him. It was not his looks or charm; both were evident, but his story of adopting his Hispanic daughter moved me to my core.

Many years ago, his middle daughter went to the hospital for minor heart surgery, and her roommate was a young girl from Mexico. She had been brought from Mexico for hip surgery. There was no family with her. He and his wife and daughter became very close with her. Before his daughter left the hospital, the doctor and nurse asked him and his wife if they would consider taking the young girl home with them for a short time, as her birth family was not financially able to. Of course, that would be fine. They all got along, and taking her home would be temporary.

Wrong. Her stay was permanent. Everyone wanted it that

way, and her eventual adoption was the outcome. In time, they were able to locate some of her biological family in Los Angeles and share her in the summers. She is grown, married, and has three children.

This story drew me to this man. I knew integrity was the fabric of his being. Moreover, here I am, the recipient of his integrity in assisted living. He is my sweetheart.

*What endearing word(s) do you use for your significant other?*

*What kindnesses have you received from your sweetheart?*

# Big Kindness

For me, wisdom in aging is the experience of Big Kindness and giving back. In 2005, I had the honor of interviewing the Buddhist monk Palden Gyatso, who had been in prison in China as a Tibetan monk for 32 years. His book, *The Autobiography of a Tibetan Monk* (1997), details his time in prison. A quote from this interview focuses on the wisdom of giving back in aging. Embodying aging is acting on the wisdom of many centuries—in giving, we receive. This is the wisdom of aging. My question to Palden Gyatso and his answer speaks this wisdom: "Do you have anything else you would like to share about aging, death, and dying?"

My final thought is just like I said before. I went to prison when I was 28 years old, and when I came out, I was 61 years old, all gray hair. When I was 61, I was released from prison and came to Dharamsala, India. Now I am 75, and there is more and more gray hair every day. Acceptance rather than guilt is one of the best ways to look at aging, death, and dying. There is no way out of it. Even though the whole world might say the sun rises in the west, the sun will not rise in the west. It will always rise in the east. They are completely fooling themselves. Accept death, and wealthy people can write their will to non-government or non-profit organizations that are helping humanitarian causes. That will be a worthy act. (Heery & Richardson, 2015)

In his answer to my question, Palden focused on the essentials of living: acceptance and compassion for others. Certainly, one hears these tenets over and over in many religions and spiritual practices—Christianity, Judaism, Islam, and, in this case, Buddhism. First, acceptance is the best way to approach the experience of aging, death, and dying. Second, give some of your time and/or wealth to humanitarian causes as a form of selfless service. This is Big Kindness; When you think of others with kindness, act on your words of kindness and give to those in need.

*Have you ever experienced Big Kindness?*

*How has kindness become wisdom for you?*

# Caring for Property

It is a milestone to purchase a home and maintain the property. First, it is an expense that not everyone can afford, and if you can afford it, it is bound to still put a dent in your savings. If you build a home, you will most likely "freak out" at the costs and time it takes. Both happened to me when my husband and I built our home on the property we had purchased. A lot of money was spent in a short period, and I was not at all used to spending large amounts of money all at once. I encountered many negative experiences while the house was being built, but the positive experiences, which were also many, involved much kindness.

In the 1980s, even in northern California, hardware stores were not accustomed to women coming in to make major orders for building a house. I was the gopher, which means I shopped for the best prices and got them. Once the men at the hardware stores understood who and what I was doing, they were excited to help me and not cheat me! The house took five years to build, but it was worth the time and money. The big memory was so many of the men in the building industry helping me with honesty.

As the years passed, we could no longer maintain the property on our own and hired an incredible man, Roberto, to help us, who is with me to this day. He and his family are part of my family. We laugh and shake our heads, and he works to keep the property in the beautiful condition it deserves. He is the steward of my land. He knows much more than I do about the property and can predict what is needed. The prediction, of course, costs money, but now I am accepting of this fact. He always kindly introduces the subject of what is needed with, "Do you have a few minutes to talk?" This translates to, "Ready to care for your property and spend money?"

Yes, I trust him. Moreover, if the land could speak, it would love him! I do, too. How could I not? There is a point in kindness where love takes over. I do not know where the point is, but when one person gives so much to help you exist daily and does not stop, it becomes love. His boys come to help, and his wife makes the best guacamole in the world! We are family! We love each other with kindness.

Right now, we are having massive rain storms with much

flooding, but my land was ready, as Roberto had prepared it for just about anything! In the wind, a pole with a light in the parking area fell over. One phone call to Roberto, and, when the rains stopped for a few hours, he installed a new pole with more lights for the parking and the pathway. Then back to rain, rain, rain! How often do we get that kindness for our land? I express so much gratitude for his kindness. Yes, he is paid, but arriving under extreme circumstances is motivated by kindness, not money.

*In finding a limitation, have you found kindness?*

*Have you experienced kindness from someone helping you with your home or land?*

## *Priorities*

At about age 10, I went over to my friend Maria's house to spend Saturday. This day would be an adventure to an unknown island in South Carolina. It was easy to get to South Carolina from Savannah. Just drive over the bridge over the Savannah River, and *voila*, you are in South Carolina. Nevertheless, arriving at this unknown island was not so easy.

This island was already named Hilton Head. Maria and I were in a car with her dad and his friend, Mr. Frasier, who was developing Hilton Head. Mr. Frasier needed insurance, which is what my friend's father did. It was a business adventure with two little girls in the back seat. We giggled a lot but became leery as the car was put on a raft to get to the island.

A car on a raft, wow! However, the island was not in sight, so our laughter became a silent concern. We finally arrived on an undeveloped island with long, beautiful beaches. I had never seen wild nature, animals running freely, trees embracing the car with their limbs, and birds guiding the car into the wild island. Yes, it was wild, not the Hilton Head Island that is known now. Mr. Frasier had a vision of this island in the 1950s, which would come true and even pass his vision in 2025.

That day was a special lesson in priorities. As Mr. Frasier drove down the gorgeous but scary beach, deer jump in front of the car. Mr. Frasier kept on his sales pitch to Mr. Little about insuring this Hilton Head investment. Couldn't Mr. Little see this island with homes and hotels? No, he could only see and hear Maria and me screaming and huddling on the floor of the car as the deer kept jumping in front of the car. Maria and I began to cry in fear of the deer and this crazy car ride on the beach. We were consumed by fear. Mr. Little's solution was to tell Mr. Frasier we had to leave the island as the girls were too scared, and he could not talk us out of this fear. Mr. Frasier tried to calm us down, saying we were safe and that he needed to finish showing the island to Mr. Little for investment purposes. We did not feel safe with deer jumping closer and closer to the car. Of course, we would have none of his story, we just wanted off this crazy island and the safety of home in Savannah.

Mr. Little insisted that Mr. Frasier turn the car back to the barge, which would take us back to the land safely. Mr. Frasier surrendered but first reminded Mr. Little he was missing a financial deal of a lifetime. Mr. Little was unsure of this truth, but the safety of the two girls was his priority.

We returned safely to land with Mr. Frasier shaking his head in dismay at Mr. Little's choice. We returned home to lots of praise from the moms who were shocked we had gone there! I think Mr. Little might have taken us without the mothers' knowledge. And, what a good choice: kids' safety over financial gain. Of course, this turned out to be a huge financial success. Hilton Head is now one of the most prestigious vacation sites on the East Coast. No jumping deer on the beach.

As we grew older, Maria and I would tease her father about his missed financial opportunity. He would laugh and remind us that money was not the gain, but our safety was his biggest investment! His kindness never faltered in his decision to prioritize our safety. I am still moved by his consistency in being kind to the children over being rich.

*Have you chosen kindness over money?*

*Have you given money as an act of kindness?*

# Kindness for an Older Daddy

My father was 51 years old when I was born in 1946. I was named after his sister, Myrtle, who died from typhoid fever in 1912 at age seven. My father always had gray hair around the edges and was bald when I was a child. My mother was 10 years younger. It was extremely rare to have two girls at their ages. I knew they were older, and I was far more acquainted with the possibility of their deaths than most of my friends who had younger parents were. Awareness of the possible loss of my parents brought a deep appreciation of the present moment. They had no outstanding health problems, but my dad smoked Pall Mall cigarettes, which would eventually take his life. They did not go out a lot and were available to "be with" me and my friends while my friends' parents went out. The "be with" was a presence that I treasured then and now.

We lived near the beach every summer, and my dad took out our 16-foot wooden boat. We went fishing, skiing and picnicking. My job was to clean the boat when we got home. We had great neighbors, and the younger dad even volunteered to park the boat for my Dad. No one had to ask the neighbor. He showed up at the moment Dad needed to put the boat in the garage or the water and efficiently backed the boat up. Of course, Daddy instructed to the right or the left, but the two dads, about 15 years apart in age, had great respect for each other. There was never a mention of the age difference, but rather a silent knowing that my dad needed some help with the boat at times. Yes, Dad's age presented some physical limitations, but this kind neighbor was always there to help.

Professionally, the neighbor was a chiropractor, and Daddy was a judge. Daddy always called him "Doctor," and he called Daddy "the Judge." They were a beautiful force together—two men who loved and supported each other as dads, taking their kids skiing, picnicking, laughing, and eating burgers dropped in the sand!

Both dads are gone now, but they have left me marvelous memories and an ongoing friendship between me and the doctor's daughter. We miss our dads, yet their friendship continues through our friendship. We now live on opposite coasts of the U.S. and help each other a lot by not parking the boat too far right or too far left, always in the middle with kindness!

*Did a parent or caregiver set an example for you by enriching a friendship with kindness?*

*Do you have a friend from your childhood with whom you share memories and stories of kindness?*

# It Is Not Your Fault

In 1985, I gave birth to my only child: a boy who was 10 and a half pounds. After a long labor, the decision was made to have a C-section, as his head and my pelvis were not a match. I was exhausted and thrilled to hold my baby. I had tears of joy to hold my precious only child at age 40. Birthing a child is not easy, as any mother will tell you, and is often accompanied by many fears that something might go wrong.

It seemed like he was fine, and I was fine, but soon after the pediatrician thoroughly examined him, there was some scary information delivered. His left eye was not reflecting correctly, and there seemed to be a small cataract. What did this mean? How did this happen? What is to be done? Will my baby see? My mind was racing, and it seemed everyone else's brains were also racing, but the professionals knew I would need to take the baby to a pediatric ophthalmologist. Thankfully, my OBGYN knew of a very good one close by.

Interestingly, what remains with me from this incident is the kindness I encountered with the pediatric ophthalmologist. She explained what needed to happen: surgery to remove the cataract, patching the strong eye to strengthen the weak eye, and putting a contact lens in the left eye. With this protocol, he would have a vision from the left eye.

"Of course, we will do anything for his vision. When and where do we start?"

She referred us to her mentor, the pioneer of this surgery in San Francisco. Then she gently leaned down, put her arm around me, and whispered, "It is not your fault." I cried, and she held me for what seemed like an eternity with a kindness that healed me and built courage for what was ahead. Because of her words, I could move forward and do the work that needed to be done so my son could see without blaming myself for a developmental anomaly.

The beginning of my mothering, which could have been racked with self-blame, was instead rich with kindness. There are many things out of one's control, and this lesson is learned over and over in mothering. Some things are in your control, and those are the things a mother needs to pay full attention to, i.e., putting contact lenses in my baby's eye daily and patching his strong eye. My son, age 36, still wears a contact lens in his left eye but has played many sports because of his depth perception of two highly functioning eyes. This is truly a blessing from much diligence on everyone's part.

*Have you had the experience that something you felt was your fault was not your fault?*

*Have you had an experience of kindness with a doctor?*

## *Challenging Kindness*

One of the biggest teachers of kindness was the sports I became engaged with during my son's preteen and teen years, roughly from 1993 to 2010. I was challenged early on with my use of kindness by one of my son's baseball coaches.

It was a little league game where the parents, coaches, and players got extremely involved in each game. My son was the pitcher for the game, and after the first pitching inning, he put his mitt down and walked off the mound. His father was beside himself with questions: What was going on? There were no answers. He wanted to go home, which we did with no explanation of what happened. In terms of parenting, this moment was full of differences between me and his father. We both agreed to leave him alone and let him tell us when he was ready what had happened.

The telling of the story came a few days later from the assistant coach who shared with us that the coach uses cursing to motivate the kids and our son did not like him calling the balls he threw "shit balls," so he quit. Cursing did not inspire or motivate him!

My husband and I arranged a meeting with the coach, and then, challenging kindness emerged in full force. First, the coach informed us that our son was a potential major league baseball pitcher, but because we were not cursing him, he would never make it. We were too "soft" with him. We had to change our parenting and curse him to motivate him to do his best.

I had no personal experience to validate the coach's assertion that cursing a child moved the child further along in baseball. It was an unbelievable moment to be in the presence of someone who adamantly believed that cursing a child would further their development and that being kind to a child would hold them back from realizing their potential.

I listened and disagreed, and we said we would get back to him after reflecting on what he shared.

We contacted other parents and the assistant coach to learn that this verbal abuse was not motivating but wrecking potential players. We bonded with other parents and took action to stop the coach from cursing the kids. By then, my son had no interest in continuing baseball and had turned his attention to golf.

I continued to speak kindly to my son in all his efforts and never engaged in cursing him as a motivator. As I write this story, I tell myself what I said when it happened: "Is what this coach is saying happening?" The answer is yes!

Many people choose unkindness over kindness, and I met one in Little League.

*Has your belief in kindness ever been challenged?*

*Have you had an experience of kindness after an experience of verbal abuse?*

# Who Owns This House?

On my life's journey, I could own a vacation home. To make the monthly payments on this second home, it was a full-time rental before becoming a vacation rental. A property manager found each renter, and our trusted interviewed potential renters for approval, as the home was in a different state.

My neighbor called and fully supported a woman artist from New York. She signed a rental agreement and moved in. Within a week, the neighbor's wife called me and asked if I had signed a contract with her. Yes, I had.

She then reported a big problem: "She is a nudist, as she walks every morning naked to her mailbox. Now, my husband is very pleased, but I am not." Being a nudist was the least of our challenges. Very soon, there were issues about the rent being late. I contacted the property manager about the rent and nudity, and we got the rent, but nothing changed.

Then, she refused to pay the rent, claiming she owned the

property. I fired the property manager, hired a lawyer, and showed up at my property with documents from my lawyer. My dear friend drove me to the property and stayed in her car while I addressed the renter. She was naked, and on the wall of my living room was painted a woman with her legs open and a fire coming out of her vagina! This painting was painted directly onto my wall! I was not so shocked about her being naked, but very shocked by the painting on my wall. I told her it was not OK to paint on my walls. She informed me it was not my wall because God had informed her the house was hers.

"Pardon me? God told you my home is yours?"

"Yes, this home is mine."

"Well, in that case, your God and my lawyer will have to sort this out."

I reached into my purse and gave her my legal documents from my lawyer.

"My lawyer and your God will be speaking very soon. We will soon know who owns this home."

I did not wait for her response but left quickly and got in my friend's car outside the house. My girlfriend drove me to the house and waited for me. She started the car, and off we went, having a "can you believe" conversation that only two close women could have, with lots of laughter!

"She thinks God told her she owns your house? She was naked the whole time?"

"Yes, and I told her I own the house. So the question of who owns the house remains until her God and my lawyer converse"

Several letters from my lawyer to her God settled the matter pretty quickly. The tenant left, and I lost some rent. Once the wall was painted, the house became a vacation rental, and I could visit my wonderful home when I wanted!

*Have you ever had a challenge sharing your home with others?*

*Have you ever experienced legal kindness?*

# No Need to Fake Kindness

In the 1970s, I attended meditation retreats to gain inner peace, but outer disturbances often interrupted this pursuit. On one occasion, I was in a meditation venue of about 300 people, the majority of meditators sitting on the floor on a mat, which designated your individual space. My cushion was my boundary, not to be crossed, right?

The woman sitting next to me kept moving her cushion closer and closer to my cushion. I quietly asked her to stop because she was almost on my cushion. Tension was rising between us when I heard the meditation teacher tap the microphone and say, "See God in everyone. Keep some people at arm's length, or two arm's lengths, and then you can see God in them."

I looked across the room where chairs were against the wall for meditators, and there was one empty chair. I grabbed my cushion and quietly walked over to the empty chair. I left plenty of space for my neighbor to keep moving but not onto me! I sat peacefully on the chair with my former neighbor several arm's length away from me, and, sure enough, with this distance, kindness rose toward my former neighbor.

This story was very simple and a profound teaching for me. I was raised to be kind, which included faking how I felt. The faking would often build resentment inside of me towards the recipient of my "pretend" kindness. The concept of keeping a distance from someone with whom I feel tension has been of great assistance in being authentic to myself and not faking kindness.

I wasted much precious time doing what I call psychobabble to myself, my therapist, the person I was in tension with, and unending conversations with many friends, all attempting to make sense of the tension. Most of the time, there was no sense in the tension. This seemed impossible for me to accept until I quietly let the tension go one day.

Letting go of the need to analyze the tension I felt was a huge gift. Tension in relationships is part of relating, and just as a leaf falls from a tree with no effort, tension can fall with kindness toward self, welcoming the next moment of kindness.

*Have you experienced kindness towards yourself and other people after setting a boundary?*

*In your experience, can part of kindness be keeping a distance from negativity?*

# Childhood Innocence

My lineage is moving forward, which is a wonderful feeling. I have one grandson who, on his first birthday, had the great fortune to have his grandparents from Tennessee and California celebrate his birthday with him. So many friends have shared that there is nothing like having a grandchild. Well, I have now had the experience of being in the presence of purity and innocence with older, wiser eyes. The gift of life is precious. I know this well, as I sat in a wheelchair with healing feet for the first year of my grandson's life.

His parents are vigilant in caring for his needs, which ensures a strong, healthy attachment to both parents. What a treat for me to watch and participate in my son raising a son. There is an abundance of kindness and love shared with my grandson from everyone around him. He has yet to experience rejection, bullying, and other dark elements of living. For now, he soaks up and gives out lots of kindness. His smile and laughter capture everyone's heart. His innocence generates kindness in everyone. Yes, it is his innocence to what is in front of him that generates kindness in others.

One Friday, I was with him at the children's museum, which is full of activity stations for different ages. My grandson was busy exploring and throwing small plastic balls in a small ball pen. A slightly older boy came to the ball pen and began throwing the balls with some aggression and loud noises. I think this incident was the first time my grandson had seen this kind of aggression. His response was kindness.

After the ball was thrown with aggression by the other boy making aggressive noises, my grandson picked up a ball and threw it with intention and laughter. His response to the other boy throwing with aggression was to stay with his kind nature and enjoy ball throwing with laughter.

Throwing a small plastic ball surrounded by many colorful balls in a contained ball pen was rich with innocence: a great learning experience with shapes, colors, and physical activity.

Through Grammie's eyes, I see people's choices regarding their responses to aggression, regardless of age. The choice to maintain my grandson's gentle innocence and kindness can be used throughout his life and mine.

*Have you experienced innocence and kindness as a response to aggression?*

*Have you observed kindness in small children?*

## Secrets for Kindness

Dinners with Mom, Dad, my sister, and I would sometimes start with my sister and me eating together, and then my parents would eat together. To this day, I have no idea why it happened this way, but it did at times, and other times we would all eat together. Often, my sister would tell me she had enough food and would slide all her food onto my plate with her fork. The dialogue went like this:

"I cannot eat all that food," I would say to my sister.

"Yes, you can. If you cannot finish it, I will throw it in the garbage."

Well, just like I said, I could not finish all the food, and, just like she said, she would take my plate and clean it off into the garbage hidden in the pantry. Like clockwork, after she emptied the food in the garbage, our mom would come in from the living room where she was chatting with Dad and compliment us on cleaning our plates, which was very important because we had been told many people were dying from starvation in China. Now, I had no idea where China was nor why the Chinese were starving, but the story was to instill fear of starvation in us and make us eat all our dinner even if we did not want it.

The big secret was that the food was thrown in the garbage, which was never disclosed. I have never discussed throwing her dinner in the garbage with my sister. However, throwing food in the garbage did happen, certainly not every night, but many nights. The question is, what does this now-disclosed secret have to do with kindness?

This little secret avoided conflict, and we went down in my mother's eyes as if we were good girls for dinner. If the secret had been disclosed as adults, there would have been a good laugh by all. There was a missed opportunity to be honest and open to conflict that could have taught us how to be kind to different needs and wants.

Many years later, when I brought a boyfriend home and was asked by my parents if he had been previously married, I answered honestly, "Of course!" My father and mother were very upset with me bringing a divorced man into their home, but after harsh words were exchanged, our love for each other survived a difference, and kindness to each other won out over keeping a secret or lying.

*Have you ever kept a secret to avoid a conflict?*

*Has kindness been part of your experience in being honest about your actions?*

# Kindness in Sports

I was never much interested in sports growing up. My adult friends would find it hard to believe as I have become an avid SF Giants fan. I have attended World Series games and have had season tickets for several seasons. My present love of sports, including playing the horrible game of golf, is because of my son.

Raising a son in Northern California in the 1990s was primarily about driving a van full of soccer equipment. I was a loyal soccer mom, driving my son and friends to games and tournaments. I had no clue what the game was about. I had played a small quantity of soccer growing up, but I never really understood what it was about. Soon, I learned to scream for goals, bring Gatorade, and be very supportive, whether a win or loss happens. What was critical was being supportive of the team.

The young man who made the goals was Hispanic, and my son's position on the team was to pass the ball to him to make the goals. The two of them had a great friendship. I always ensured I got him to all the games, whether in or out of town. His parents worked a lot just to get by and could not afford to take time off for the games. They missed seeing him play. I would return him after the games to his home and was greeted by his mom with a big platter of tomales. We would share what a great job her son had done at the game. Despite my many invitations to take her to a game, his mother refused to go as she had to work. I did not trust that she had to work and was concerned she was worried about being different at the games. I tried to include her, but my efforts failed, and I continued to be the driver and recipient of great Mexican food.

    During the traveling trips, we would all share one room. Regularly, this young man would say a long prayer before he slept. I quietly asked him what he was praying for. He said that he prayed he would not hurt anyone who got in his way in making a goal. During the games, after he made a goal, he would regularly cross himself and come back to anyone he had hit along his route to the goal. He would ask if they were ok and apologize for knocking them down. It was amazing to watch this young man not only make goals but make sure that he did not harm anyone in the process.

## Small Kindness

I have been thinking about the way when you walk

down a crowded aisle, people pull their legs

to let you by. Or how strangers still say "bless you"

when someone sneezes....

Only these brief moments of exchange.

What if they are the true dwelling of the holy, these

fleeting temples we make together when we say, "Here,

have my seat," "Go ahead — you first," "I like your hat."

Danusha Laméris (2019)

*Has playing or watching a sport brought you the experience of kindness?*

*Have you ever experienced kindness as holy?*

# Kindness Delivered to Jealousy

I suffered terribly from jealousy as a young child. I always thought that what my older sister had was what I should have as a very special friend, As on my report card, almost everything that I did not have.

I tried to be like her and her friends, but I failed miserably at the effort. Often, I would bring them Cokes in hopes they would invite me to stay and listen to them, which never happened. Instead, I sat still next to the closed door of their room and listened to as much as I could without being discovered. However, all the listening and repeating what they said did not help either. I was shy in those days and pretty much stayed to myself, asking deeper questions that no one wanted to engage with, such as, "Where did I come from?"

This desire to be someone else created a deep jealousy accompanied by a feeling that something was missing in me. I did not know what, but these longings to be accepted and like everyone else were even bigger than my questions of existence. My feelings of jealousy won out, and they did not resolve until I was much older and had engaged in psychotherapy. Then, I began to like the skin I was born in and the complex feelings I had under my skin.

In my journey of becoming, accepting, and loving myself, I had the honor to meet an Indian teacher in London. After he had given a talk on meditation in a quiet garden, he walked around and chatted. I was standing in a small group listening to him when he turned toward me and out of nowhere said the following, as his eyes looked deeply into my eyes: "Jealous. If you break the word down, it is *'jea'* or *'jai'* in French, and I am. Then *'lous'* or *'lousy'* in English. Translation of jealous is I am lousy."

He smiled very kindly at me and walked off. When someone heard what he said, they looked at me and asked what that was about.

I have suffered from jealousy most of my life. His words were for me. I have never fully understood my jealousy, but his truthful words delivered with such kindness have brought me insight and relief. Truth can be hard or kind or a little of both. Perhaps his words were a little of both. I became dedicated, when I felt jealous, to looking closely at feeling lousy about me. Who needs that feeling? Nobody, including me!

It was a long transformation journey, but those kind eyes, repeatedly delivering this truth to me, were a great motivator for releasing my jealousy.

*Have kind words brought insight into a negative pattern you have had?*

*Have you experienced jealousy and had kindness help you through this emotion?*

## *Piled Higher and Deeper With Kindness*

There is an old saying behind the title Ph.D., known as "Piled Higher and Deeper." The first time I heard this saying, I was about four years in the process of getting my Ph.D. in psychology. It was too late to quit, and I still held hope that the process was worth the struggle.

Yes, getting a Ph.D. is a struggle. First, there are the required courses, some having nothing to do with what I would eventually do but rather a measure of my tolerance to material that did not interest me. There was material that did interest me and professors who inspired me. Then, I chose a topic to research for a dissertation and got the administration's approval. Then, I formed a committee of three professors to support me through my research and dissertation writing.

During this time, I had a profound dream or perhaps a visit from a dear friend who had died about two years before the dream. In the dream, my friend Vincent called my name and told me he had gone nowhere; to listen, he was everywhere. Then, a piercing sound came into the bedroom, and I felt Vincent's presence all over the room. My husband awoke at this time and asked, "What is that sound?" I could hardly speak as tears rolled down my face. I said Vincent had come into the room through this sound. Hard to believe, but we both believed. Of course, we got up, and I searched over and over for the meaning of this experience. I had not decided on the research topic for my dissertation, but there it was: the experience of hearing voices. This experience was the beginning of research on normal people, that is, people who had not been diagnosed with a mental disorder such as schizophrenia who heard voices. This experience was my guidance through my research.

The administration approved the topic, and I formed a committee. One of the members I chose for my committee was my dear mentor, who had published articles, chapters, and books. I mistakenly thought he would be of assistance in this process. Well, he was and was not. He used a green ink pen to make corrections to my writings, and each page was full of green ink. I interviewed thirty people not diagnosed with a mental disorder, and the results of my research were vibrant. But my mentor's judgments were as rich as the material. In retrospect, he was delivering kindness, putting my cutting-edge research into the best possible written form.

At first, I thought his judgments were beneficial, but then the judgments just kept coming, and there was no end to his judgments. Nothing I wrote was good enough. The chair of my committee, a strong woman with numbers from a German concentration camp on one wrist, had enough of his corrections, as she wanted the dissertation signed by all members and for me to publish a paper on my findings. I could not kick him off the committee, so I decided to give up on the dissertation and publish the findings with the chair of my committee.

I went to my mentor's office with the 300-plus pages of the dissertation, ready with my decision. He sat in his chair holding his green ink pen, eager to make judgments. I kept standing and said the following: "I have decided I do not want to be in the Piled Higher Deeper Club and will be publishing my research with my chair on my own. I have had enough of your green ink." I then tossed the three hundred-plus pages into the air, and they fell slowly to the floor. To my surprise, he got on his knees on the floor and found the signature page of the dissertation. He signed the signature page and gave it to me. Silence and tears were present.

He took me to the bookshelves where he had his and others' published books. He opened several published books, all full of green ink on each page.

"I never stop with my critical voice. Thank you for stopping me," he said with kindness.

We hugged, cried, and laughed together. The dissertation was signed by all committee members, a paper was published on my work, and I made many presentations on my findings.

A presentation in Holland had many diagnosed schizophrenic patients and psychiatrists present. Everyone was so grateful for my research. There were many thank-yous and applause for validating that hearing voices could be helpful, not destructive.

*Have you stopped someone criticizing you and experienced kindness from them?*

*Have you ever experienced judgment with kindness?*

# *Luck*

When someone leaps to work independently, it takes a lot of courage, smarts, fortitude, and luck. I have found that when luck visits me, kindness appears, as the two seem to accompany each other. As I receive luck, another may or may not. One door may open for me and shut for another. This experience is common in self-employment.

When I lived in Germany, I wanted so badly to live and work in Holland. Finally, I thought I had found the door that would open to work in Holland. My husband and I pursued giving a lecture at a renowned growth clinic in Amsterdam. We prepared for months for this lecture. Arriving early that evening, we set up the room and waited. No one came. Finally, one very quiet woman came into the room a little late.

We laughed a bit about presenting to one person but proceeded to do so. Then, about 15 minutes into the evening, a very tall, distinguished woman arrived. She sat down and apologized for her late arrival. We proceeded, and at the end, I gave what I referred to as a guided deep relaxation experience. After this experience, the two women were very impressed and wanted to know more about our work.

The late arrival shared that she had awakened from a nap, started reading the brochure about our presentation, and bolted out of her house to come. Now she knew why. This relaxation experience was exactly what she was looking for. She was organizing the yearly conference for hypnosis and needed someone to give an experience of relaxation over a microphone to over 400 people. Would I be interested? It only takes one person. This evening was the beginning of a very successful career in Amsterdam. This woman could not restrain her kindness to us in every step of the process of setting up our work, introducing us to clinicians, and more.

*Where have you experienced kindness in your professional world?*

*Have you given kindness to someone at the beginning of their career?*

# Once Upon a Time

Once upon a time, a most beautiful woman lived in Oklahoma. Many aspects of her life seem like a fairy tale, so I will continue to present her story and my relationship with her as a fairy tale.

She lived a simple life with her husband and two small children, working part-time to pay the bills. Then, she received a phone call from an attorney in Manhattan.

He asked her to verify her identity and if she had a distant male cousin in New York.

"Well, I think I do, but very distant. I think I met him a few times."

"Yes," the attorney said, "you are the woman we are looking for. You need to come to Manhattan as soon as possible. Your cousin has died, and we need to read you his will in person. We will send you an airline ticket immediately."

"What? Me? Go to Manhattan to hear a will? Can't you just

tell me the will over the phone?"

The attorney was very adamant that disclosing the will to her had to be in person.

"Well, I will need to discuss this matter with my husband. I have never been to Manhattan and certainly not by myself."

Again, the attorney was adamant that she needed to come as soon as possible. He would call her the next day after she spoke with her husband.

The conversation with her husband was brief, and they both agreed that she should go.

Why not? She had met this cousin and knew he lived in Manhattan, and it was a free trip.

Details were arranged, and she arrived at the attorney's office in Manhattan in a few days. She settled into a big chair across from the attorney, who proceeded to read her cousin's will to her. He did not have any immediate family. He described in his will that she was the most beautiful person that he had ever met and could never get her out of his mind and heart. He wanted her to know how much he appreciated her beauty by leaving her all of his money in hopes it would bring her great joy.

This cousin owned oil wells in Oklahoma and was worth billions. She was the inheritor of all his wealth.

"What? Are you sure?" she leaned forward and asked the attorney. "Are these his wishes?"

"Yes. I am one hundred per cent."

It seemed like a dream or the quirky afternoon show The Millionaire, which aired on TV. The theme was giving away a million dollars to unknown people with the agreement that they would not tell where they received the money.

This story was different. There was no stipulation that she could not tell anyone. It was much more than a million and would continue to grow in value. The money was a gift to her because her beautiful face had brought this man so much joy that he wanted to return that joy by giving her his money at his death.

I first heard the story from my best friend, one of her granddaughters. She invited me to visit this "lucky" beautiful grandmother with her in Oklahoma. I could not believe this story, but I could believe it was a fairytale. So, sure, let us go meet her wealthy grandmother. Off we went, driving to visit her grandmother in Oklahoma.

We arrived at a beautiful yet simple home in a very expensive part of town. Driving up her driveway, I noticed a significant car—a Rolls Royce. This car foreshadowed what was to emerge.

Grannie was drop-dead beautiful. Simple clothes, smooth

skin, sparkling eyes, wavy gray hair, and a smile that went forever across her beautiful face. As I stepped into her home, it felt very surreal. This beautiful woman lived alone in her old years and had only a driver to come once in a while to take her out in her Rolls Royce.

We had tea and were shown to our delightful rooms, which overlooked a colorful garden. The rooms had two big twin beds and large comfy pillows, a setting for a good book and a long sleep, which we did immediately.

The next morning, we ate breakfast leisurely in the garden, served by a delightful woman who cooked all our meals. Grannie informed us that the driver was sick and wanted us to see her town, so would I be so kind as to be our driver for the day?

"Who? Me? Drive your Rolls Royce?"

Her huge smile, accompanied by a heart-filled laugh, answered my question.

Yes, I would drive her Rolls Royce, and Grannie and my friend would sit in the back. It was official when she handed me a driver's cap for my head!

The drive around town was the first of many I quickly became accustomed to and greatly enjoyed! Was it a dream? No, I was driving a Rolls Royce with a driver's hat to define my position!

One quiet evening, after reading together in the parlor, Grannie closed her book and said she had a great idea.

What if we stayed longer with her and I could be her driver?

After graduating from college, I was on my way to California to start my career in a field I did not know. My plans were vague, but living in Oklahoma and driving Ms. Grannie in her Rolls somehow did not fit the picture my parents or I had of a college graduate!

I jumped from my chair and gave her a big hug, realizing how much her kindness had meant to me. I learned that being rich and beautiful can be real, not just a fairy tale. Onward to California, I went!

*Have you ever experienced kindness from a wealthy person?*

*Can you find kindness in the surprising experiences in your life?*

## *Magical Mistake*

I attended the opera Tosca at the Royal Opera House in London in the 1990s. I was very fortunate that Pavarotti was the main performer. My dear friend Roger secured two tickets and offered me one.

Offering me one opera ticket brought me so much joy. Roger remembered my story of growing up with opera with my mom and wanted me to experience Pavarotti singing opera. We did not have to sit together, but that was not important. We figured out where to meet outside after the performance and found our seats. My seat was great, and I settled into the most incredible opera performance in the most incredible surroundings ever. There was applause throughout the performance and a standing ovation at the end. I felt I had been lifted by Pavarotti's voice to deep serenity. It was magic.

Then I gathered my things, which included the 35mm camera that I had used that day touring London. The people leaving were pushing hard, and then a man in front of me pointed with his arm to turn right to some stairs, which I did, thinking this would be a quicker exit. It was not. I had no idea where I was, and I was faced with narrow stairs leading up to who knows where. Then I heard the words, "Welcome, Mr. Prime Minister!" What? Who was in front of me and where was I? Sure enough, Prime Minister John Major and his wife were in front of me. I asked the man at my side where the stairs led. He answered, "Hurry along. You are with the press, correct?" He pointed to the 35mm around my neck, and I finally understood that I had been mistaken for the press. Do I head up the stairs as a mistaken press or come clean with the fact that I am an American tourist?

With great regret that I would not be in the same room with Pavarotti, I said,

"There has been a mistake, I am an American tourist; I do not belong to the press."

"Well, follow me quickly," he said, realizing he was part of creating this mistake.

I followed him out of the stairwell and onto the busy, cold London street. He waved me goodbye with a smile of kindness. It was as if my truth-telling had saved him from a big embarrassment. I had come so close yet so far to the magical voice!

*Has honesty been part of your experience of kindness?*

*Have you ever experienced kindness in a place you were not supposed to be?*

# Dining With Kindness

In January 2016, I traveled to Argentina to visit longtime friends. Before meeting up with my friends, who were incredible hosts, I traveled alone and experienced so much kindness. Perhaps being an older woman traveling alone was the reason I received so much kindness, but whatever the reason, I soaked it up.

I booked a table for one in a very well-known restaurant on Saturday night in Mendoza, where the famous Malbec red wine is made. My hotel arranged a cab for me, and I arrived safely at the restaurant to be seated at a table a nice distance from other tables. Immediately, in perfect English, my waiter introduced himself and poured me a sample of their best Malbec. As I sipped this delicious wine, he announced that if I liked it, he would be glad to show me the wine cellar where it was stored. Well, of course, I was eager to go.

As I stood up, I noticed a couple watching me who appeared

to be Americans and smiled as I moved to join the waiter in the wine cellar. As we walked to the wine cellar, he showed me all the beautiful gardens belonging to the restaurant and shared the heritage of this Michelin restaurant. I was in awe of the details of the restaurant, gardens, and people. Moreover, now, down we went to the immense cellar. What a joy to see hundreds of bottles of the best Malbec! There were a couple of bottles opened, and he poured me a taste, explained it in detail, and delighted my palate. We came to the end of the cellar tour and returned to my table, where he described the menu in detail and his suggestions for the best way to order. I followed his suggestions and settled into another glass of Malbec to wait for my food.

The American couple sitting next to me immediately wanted to know all about the wine cellar, so I shared my experience. Then, we proceeded to ask each other questions. Why were they there? They were on their honeymoon from San Diego, California. The wife had lots of questions. They asked me about traveling alone, including how I got to this wine cellar. I shared that I felt very comfortable traveling alone in Argentina, and the people, including this waiter, were all very kind to me.

She turned to her new husband and said, "Would it be OK with you if I went to a very nice restaurant tomorrow night by myself? I would love to see an Argentine wine cellar, and I think it will happen if I am alone."

"Of course," he said. "I agree, but I want to be in the restaurant to watch."

We raised our glasses to toast single women eating alone and visiting wine cellars! We laughed and continued chatting throughout our neighbor dinners.

Did I dine alone? Not really. I dined with kindness from neighbors and the waiter.

*Have you dined alone and experienced kindness?*

*What have you done out of the box, and was kindness part of that experience?*

# Gift of Kindness

My niece has always been very special to me. I have been known as the aunt who lived in the faraway land of California, coming to visit on special occasions. One Christmas, my husband and I arrived unannounced. We took a taxi from the airport, and before we arrived at my sister's home on Christmas day, we wrapped ourselves in Christmas paper! My family was surprised and delighted.

We had the great intention of getting my niece a real puppy and, as a space holder, gave her a remote-controlled dog for Christmas. She had wanted a puppy for a long time. Putting it mildly, her mom and dad did not support this idea. However, my love of dogs and my rebellious nature propelled me into action.

After Christmas, I spent one-on-one time with my brother-in-law, discussing a puppy for his daughter. He was not opposed but warned me that my sister was, whom I chose not to discuss this subject with, knowing it would go nowhere and prevent it from happening. I talked with my niece about her wanting a puppy; her excitement about this possibility stole my heart. I could not resist her even promising to care for the dog! I proceeded to look in the newspaper for puppies for sale, and sure enough, two small Schnauzer puppies named Chevis and Regal were for sale. My husband and I went to check them out and how cute they were. We paid for Chevis and arranged to come back and get Chevis for my niece's sixth birthday on January 1.

This gift of kindness was for my niece, certainly not for her parents, who would be caring for this cute puppy. I hoped they would fall in love with Chevis, which happened over a long period and became the glue of my small Georgia family. In the meantime, the giving of the puppy and then leaving for California the next day caused quite a scene in my family. It was the icing on the cake of how strange the California sister and daughter were, right?

When my family took us to the airport, they locked Chevis downstairs at my mother's house, and Chevis proceeded to eat all the carpet in the stairwell! Upon returning from the airport and letting him outside, he hid from my brother-in-law and tried to bite him. The beginning was awful, to put it mildly, but my niece was in love, and soon to follow was my brother-in-law's love. My mother and sister were very slow to come around, but he truly was the love of everyone's life in time. Eventually, a little gratitude came my way. My kindness to my niece won out in the end, with my brother-in-law washing him at my mom's house and caring for him in his old age with so much love.

Kindness took courage beyond the circumstances at the time.

*Have you ever given a gift of kindness that was not wanted?*

*How do you define kindness?*

## Money Kindness

What is money kindness? It is giving back when the giving is appropriate. Appropriate? Who decides, and how much is appropriate? Today, tips are calculated for you on the credit card charger: push a button to leave 10, 15, 20 or 25 percent. This is instant money kindness.

During a life of over 78 years, there are many instances where money kindness comes up as a choice, with no machine calculating the amount for me to give. It is my choice to give or ignore money kindness. Yes, the opportunity to give can be ignored. What about choosing to give and then feeling the amount is insufficient, and going back to give more?

There have been many times I have frequented a laundromat. Most of these visits occurred when I was in college or renting an apartment. Once I owned my home, I only visited the laundromat when my machine(s) were broken. When a dear friend from Georgia was visiting me in California, the dryer broke, so off we went with wet clothes to the laundromat. When there is no money change machine in a laundromat, there is plenty of opportunity to ask and receive change from fellow customers, but this is not the money kindness that happened that day. We had the correct change, loaded the dryers with our wet clothes, and were off for a delicious dinner at a nearby restaurant. Of course, we forget the clothes. What older adult homeowner goes to a laundromat after dinner? When I got home and searched for my pajamas; I remembered we had left the clothes at the laundromat. My friend said, "No, do not go now," I proceeded alone to the laundromat in a sketchy neighborhood. I knocked on the locked door. A man inside turned on a light and unlocked the front door. A kind soul who immediately said, "You forgot your clothes, right?"

With earned humility, I said, "Right, and thank you for opening the door."

"I folded them, and here they are," he said, guiding me toward the neatly folded clothes.

I could hardly believe my eyes; what kindness from a stranger.

"What do I owe you?" I asked, expecting a heavy fee.

"Nothing, glad I could be of service in saving your nice clothes."

"Oh no, I must give you something for your work."

"One cup of coffee will do."

"Maybe you can get two cups," handing him $5 and thanking him as I proceeded in the dark to my car with folded clothes.

He smiled and locked the door. As I put my car in reverse and turned around, I wondered how much the folded clothes were worth.

I turned the car around, parked, went to the front door, knocked, and he opened the door, asking if I had forgotten something.

"Yes, I am paying you for what you did." I handed him a $20 bill.

"No, missy, you do not need to do this."

"Yes, I do, and I will. Thanks again, bye!"

Remembering to tip has been and continues to be part of my living with delicious kindness.

*Have you ever tipped extra for a person who showed you kindness?*

*What small events in your life are examples of kindness?*

## Kindness Meets Judgment

When I was in graduate school, I waited tables part of the time to support myself financially. I highly recommend this profession to everyone. It is in this stage of serving others that I experienced kindness meeting judgment with unmatched power.

My waitressing supervisor, Shirley, had 30 years of experience and brought wisdom to many diverse challenges. She imparted her wisdom to me with incredible kindness every time I worked. A bustling, successful Northern California restaurant with huge diversity was about as far from my privileged Southern roots as I could get. It was time to get street-smart and earn a living. Moreover, that I did!

As I straightened my yellow, short, dress uniform in the kitchen, Shirley winked at me and put her arm around me. Words were not necessary. Her support was palpable. I felt confident, but I was also nervous. I had already served a couple of tables and knew my anxiety gave me an edge that helped, but little did I know what was going to happen at this table. It was an older couple who were very polite and curious about what was on the menu that night. As I was explaining the menu, the owner's wife, who usually sat at the bar, walked up to the table and proceeded to trash me in front of the customers.

She spoke very loudly, so many people in the restaurant heard her words of disdain for me. Her presence reeked of alcohol as she bellowed out. I was new but extremely slow and did not understand anything about the restaurant business—perhaps I never would! I ran from the table back to the kitchen with tears streaming down my face, to be met by determined Shirley, who grabbed me by the shoulders.

"Listen to me, this is your opportunity for a huge tip! Wipe those tears and go back to the table. They are going to ask you why you are working here and receiving this abuse. Cock your head." Which I did. "No, more. Almost to your left shoulder, look pathetic! Good. Then, say in your Southern accent that you must work because you have to pay for graduate school, and then look at the woman, not the man. The woman will get your attention, so make eye contact with her. She will then tell you your situation is awful and you should leave. She will give you much motherly advice. Be grateful and refocus on their order. OK, stand straight and tall. You are on the road for big tips. After you leave their table, the woman is going to tell the man to tip you big, which he will do. You will get screamed at infrequently by the same woman who drinks a lot. Her trashing you is an opportunity to make money, and that is why you are here, got it?"

Internally, I was shocked. I thought she would tell me to leave the restaurant, but her wisdom was to stay the course and reap the benefits! Sure enough, I did as she instructed and got a tip of $50! Not only that night, but the couple returned almost every Friday and left me $50! We got to know each other, and I enjoyed their financial and emotional support. Who would have thought? Perhaps those who have lived longer would have all known that kindness is eager to meet judgment. My waitress job became a true teacher in human behavior.

*Have you experienced kindness after you have received negative judgment?*

*How is kindness a part of your daily life?*

## Healers

In my lifetime, healers have come in many forms to me: acupuncturists, caregivers, doctors, family, friends, nurses, occupational therapists, paramedics, physician assistants, physical therapists, physical trainers, psychics, psychotherapists, and teachers. After falling down my home steps and breaking my left ankle and right foot at age 75, I had the honor of being in the presence of many healers.

First, there was my son, whom I called and said, "I fell and think I broke at least one foot."

"Mom, hang up. I am calling 911!"

The ambulance was at my door within minutes. The kindest paramedics asked me questions, including my name, age, date of birth, and who the president was. A dear friend also came out to make sure the ambulance had arrived. My answers were all good, and off we went to the hospital, where my son and dear sweetheart were waiting outside the emergency room.

Paramedics rolled me to the front of the line because of my age and the severity of my accident. Everyone in the ER was kind, holding my hand, assuring me I would be fine, and checking my vitals and memory with the usual questions.

I teased them a little after many of the same questions; I said the year I was born was 2024! They looked at me seriously, and I laughed and encouraged some humor to counteract the monotonous questions they had to ask. They joined me in laughing, and we moved forward with lightness to the severe physical condition.

Everything moved quickly and slowly. That is, I had to wait, sleep, wait, and finally be seen by the doctor with scheduled surgery. As I waited in my room, a most remarkable man came and picked up the trash, singing a gospel song as he worked. I thanked him for taking the trash, and he looked up and said,

Ma'am, I am honored to keep your room clean to assist your healing. I tell my children daily we are here to serve, to serve with kindness."

He looked at me with so much kindness and quietly left with the trash. Tears streamed down my face as I began my journey into humility. I slept deeply that night, knowing I had many kind hands in my healing. The surgeries were successful but not easy. I had the very best orthopedic surgeon, nurses, and anesthesiologists, all attentive and kind. Yes, this is their job, but it is very stressful with many demands, yet all the people who helped me never faltered in being present in my healing process.

Then there are the physical and occupational therapists who got me on my feet, and with a walker, I began to walk again! The occupational therapist was from Georgia and grew up in Athens, home to the University of Georgia. When she became my OT, I knew I had help from my parents, who lived and died in Georgia. Our Southern accents and humor about everything sped up the healing.

When I moved home, I had home help from one amazing woman caring for all my daily functions, a PT and an OT coming three times a week, and an acupuncturist coming once a week, all healing with kindness. The acupuncturist would work on me and leave quietly as I slept on my bed from the session.

Now, I drive to a PT and acupuncturist's office. A big step: driving after I recovered from "institutional fear" created by living in rehabilitation in a room by myself for three months. There was my small wonderful family and friends visiting me, but the isolation and inability to walk brought fear of functioning outside the walls of rehabilitation.

My sweetheart and I would have a glass or two of wine late afternoon at a table outside, which we called "Myrtle's Café"!

Friends would visit with flowers and gifts of books, delicious food, a list of the best Netflix shows to watch, and funny life stories! However, there was a good dose of isolation that left fears of being out in the world when I returned home. These fears showed up slowly as I moved into the world. I stayed close to home and slowly familiarized myself with my car by sitting and holding the steering wheel, but not starting the car. Finally, courage returned, and I drove with confidence.

My walking came back slowly but steadily with so much help and support from my sweetheart, my son, daughter-in-law, friends, caregiver, acupuncturist, PT, and prayers from my college roommates from 55 years ago, and friends I had known since kindergarten! I have kept the cards of kindness from so many people near and far. Kindness was the true healer.

*Have you experienced kindness during a physical recovery?*

*How have you returned kindness to those who helped you through challenging times?*

# In Gratitude to All My Caregivers

I have tried to put into words my deepest gratitude to my caregivers. I hope this poem expresses a small amount of my gratitude.

Jesus' Hands

I know kindness

In my aging

I have met so many caregivers

None are white

Each from a different country

Changing my soiled diapers

Rolling me over

With so much care

Their hands caress

My broken feet

With warm water

Yes, it is Jesus

So many Jesuses

Washing my feet

With Kindness

With Kindness

—M Heery

## Somewhere Over the Rainbow

About two months into living in rehab with my broken feet, I read on the internet that Yo-Yo Ma, the renowned cellist was coming to the Green Center in Sonoma County, where I live. The tickets went on sale for an April 2023 date in August of 2022. I got two tickets, not together but not far apart. The event was sold out. I have listened to Yo-Yo Ma for many years, and now, at rehab, I ask Alexa to play him daily. His music healed me emotionally and brought me so much inner peace. I moved from worrying about my feet to a deep sense of letting go and leaning into an appreciation of the people caring for me, the delicious food, and the beautiful garden I had the privilege of watching grow from my bedroom window. I told myself I would be walking in April of 2023, and I would get to see Yo-Yo Ma.

I walked into the Green Center in April of 2023 with the help of one walking stick and, of course, my dear friend, whose arm I held as needed. Our seats were separate, and the lovely woman

I shared the box seats with had fallen two days before and sprained her wrist. We chatted, finding out how much music meant to both of us and how it was part of our healing. She shared that when she saw the doctor two days ago, she told him that no matter what, she was going to see Yo-Yo Ma. Moreover, there she was, sitting next to me, who had fallen and broken both feet 10 months ago. We laughed and shared some happy and sad stories of our 75 years of living. The connection was easy, sensitive, and powerful for both of us.

When Yo-Yo Ma came on stage and placed his hand over his heart, the theater was filled with joy. We listened to Yo-Yo Ma in silence and awe. The music moved me, but it was not until the second encore that my heart fully opened, and I wept.

> Somewhere over the rainbow
> Skies are blue
> And the dreams that you dare to dream
> Really do come true
> — Arlen & Harburg (1939)

Kindness was all over Yo-Yo Ma's face as he played this piece and the whole concert. Sitting next to me, my new friend and I hugged with a knowingness that we had been put together to share in our healing through music, which frequently heals.

I had dared to dream of walking into Yo-Yo Ma's performances in April and August with healing feet; my dream came true. I will never stop dreaming. I want this piece to be played at my Celebration of Life. This music brings hope for something new and positive somewhere over the rainbow.

*What dream have you dreamt that came true?*

*Have you shared your hand with a stranger in kindness?*

# Ground Transportation

I have traveled extensively in my life, including Europe, Russia, Turkey, Iran, Afghanistan, Pakistan, India, Canada, Mexico, Thailand, Bhutan, China, Hong Kong, Bali, Taiwan, Argentina, Ecuador, the Galapagos Islands, Costa Rica, and across the United States. In my travels, I tended to use ground transportation, such as taxis, Ubers, buses, and trains. These experiences included so much kindness from both the people operating the transportation and using it.

Often, I would not know the language but would have the address I was going to in writing. When I showed someone the address, they would tell me where to get off the train or bus and how to proceed once off the public transportation. Sometimes, they even went as far as to announce over the speaker, "Time for the American girl to get off!" People would laugh and look at me because I was the only American! The giggles were often accompanied by, "Do you want me to escort you?" This question came often in Turkey; women without burkas were unsafe. However, I learned to cover my head in Turkey and wear a long skirt and sleeves. Furthermore, I would still accept the offers to assist me when I got off the bus. With the volunteer assisting me, always a man, he would shout out loud in Turkish, "Out of the way, important visitor!"

"I am only going to the market," I would tell him.

His response: "Yes, purchasing food for you and your family is very important."

These times were very rare, as I mostly went to the market with my husband out of fear of strangers and what might happen to me. Reflecting on these experiences using ground transportation, I realize that when I stepped outside of my fear, asked questions, and wrote out the addresses of where I was going, I was met with kindness. I was reminded that strangers are humans who want to connect with mutual kindness. Strangers responded to my questions, sincere smile, and kindness I expressed by putting my hand over my heart and saying thank you to all the fantastic strangers who helped me.

*Have you experienced kindness using ground transportation?*

*Has kindness been part of moving through a fear you have had?*

# *Imagination and Kindness*

I developed an active imagination when a very close friend of my mom's brought me small gifts from different parts of the world she visited. She had no children, and I became her daughter through these infrequent visits. I called her aunt and kept all her small gifts in a drawer next to my bed. Over the years, I would imagine each place she told me the gift had come from. I decided every time she brought me a gift that I would one day travel to some of these faraway places. In the meantime, I would imagine them. As I grew, my imagination of faraway places became a reality.

In college, I traveled to Vienna to study art and music. My roommate was African American, and she took me to an all-black jazz club in Vienna for our evening entertainment. Being the only white person in the club opened my eyes and heart to being different and accepted. I was unsure if I would be accepted, but I soon realized that the only requirement was love of the music, nothing else. The club participants were from all over the world and loved listening to live jazz. I loved the music, and I was in with laughter and new friends.

After graduating from college, I returned to Europe with my childhood friend, Eileen. Her father bought her a Peugeot station wagon in France, which we drove all over Europe and Morocco. Were we crazy? YES! In Morocco, every hotel employee helped us with when and where to go out and how to stay safe. All the strangers we met were welcoming and protective. We were lucky and soon learned to leave Morocco for safer ground in Europe, where 20-year-old girls can travel!

After Europe, we visited Eileen's sister in Vermont and stayed. I worked on a local paper and became the question girl. I asked people questions at ski resorts, took their pictures, skied, and returned to the paper's office to put the photos, questions, and answers in the paper. Moreover, friends would come to visit to witness the ski life Eileen and I were living in Vermont.

One friend was a medical student in Georgia and arrived in Vermont to do unimaginable research with us. He managed to bring some marijuana and wanted to test our physical reactions to the marijuana, i.e., heart rate, dilation of eyes, and hallucinations. We were in for the research and smoked some of the marijuana with the researcher. My heartbeat and eye dilations stayed normal, but the researcher saw fire coming out of my head and started hitting my head to put out the imagined fire. There was no fire coming out of my head, only in his imagination! We started belly laughs for a long time until we all drifted off into corners of the house and slept off our stoned state of mind.

This story of my doctor friend has been embellished through everyone's imagination over the years. I am sure I am reporting an embellished version, but even without embellishment, the story is humorous and innocent. These traveling stories are all rich with innocence and the kindness of others helping me by bringing my imagination into reality.

*Have you ever manifested a childhood dream into reality as an adult?*

*What are your experiences of kindness from others?*

## On Her Tongue Is the Law of Kindness

My Aunt Lucille always spoke with kindness. I call her tongue the law of kindness. She lived in a small southern Georgia town with Uncle Billy and her mother, whom she cared for until she died. My childhood memory of her is red lipstick and red fingernail polish, which were outrageous in the 1950s. I remember running down the stairs of the beach house and flying into her arms when she and Uncle Billy would come to visit, which was not often.

They did not have children, and Aunt Lucille and I became close, like mother and daughter. She would read books to me, comb my hair, and giggle about all kinds of stories with me. We were connected and stayed connected throughout my childhood. I have no clue if she ever went to college, but she had a degree in kindness.

When I returned to Georgia for visits, I regularly visited Aunt Lucille. Her town had a church on each corner and one wonderful restaurant that served the best lobster bisque. My son loved visiting her and the absolute simplicity of her home and town.

We would stay about two hours, reviewing our family's history and sharing stories from my childhood. It always amazed me how many positive stories she remembered. It was as if the negative things that did happen left her, and her tongue spoke only kindness of all the family, including my grandmother, who lived with her for a while and became pretty much an entitled grand dame at her age.

We would laugh about the orders she took from Grannie as she never felt insulted but rather had patience in caring for her aging mother-in-law, whose life was living with her son and daughter-in-law in a tiny town in southern Georgia. It was not the busy life she had been used to in the big city of Savannah.

My son would sit quietly in the car returning from Aunt Lucille's visit, soaking up the love he had received and the knowledge of his extended southern family: A lived experience of ancestors, not just reading about ancestors on the internet.

*Do you remember kindness from an older relative?*

*Do you keep in contact with your extended family?*

## Self-Kindness

Being kind to myself is a long journey in my life. Until recently, the "could have" or "should have," a self-critic voice spoke loudly in my head. I am pondering how I got control of my self-critic and turned toward the kind voice that says I am just fine; everything is emerging as it should, with perfections and imperfections. Yes, there are regrets I have in living and also many kindnesses in living. Are they about even? No, I can honestly say I have more kindnesses.

My different professions, including teaching psychology and individual and couples psychotherapy, have taught me much about the critical voice and how it manifests for others. The power of the critic can be arrested with self-kindness, but vigilance is very important. One assignment I give students and clients with powerful self-critical voices is to take five minutes, sit, close your eyes, and count to five on the inhale and fifteen on the exhale. Just five minutes once a day. If they find they like it, I encourage them to try twice a day, and, if they like it, I encourage them to go for 10 minutes a day. This simple exercise brings one close to enjoying the kindness of the moment, with nothing to do, nowhere to go, just sitting, maybe with a gentle smile, if that feels right.

I practice this simple exercise regularly, especially when the critical voice becomes active about being a mother. In addition to my breathing, I remind myself of facts, such as who my son has become: a very happy young man happily married with an three-year-old son and a wonderful job and home. He became himself as I always encouraged, but, as he reminds me, he was raised by two psychologists, implying he became who he became both because of and in spite me. Interestingly, this is exactly what my mother said: "You became who you are in spite of me."

Self-criticism is extreme when it comes to motherhood. I wanted to be different from my mother, but here I am with my grown son, who is becoming himself partially in spite of me. What goes around comes around! Self-kindness is so important, as I know my son, and I appreciate and love each other deeply. I know this fact when we end our phone chats with, "I love you." Life is fragile, and loving kindness needs expression.

*Have you ever used self-kindness to manage your self-criticism?*

*What do you do for self-kindness?*

## *First Grade*

Ms. Cook was my first-grade teacher. She seemed 80 years old with 80-year-old ideas. I am left-handed, and she soon informed me that left-handed people are stupid. Innocently, I asked what did stupid mean?

"Something you do NOT want to be. You will need to stay at your desk during recess and work on writing with your right hand."

I did and was pretty successful at my tireless efforts, but I had no friends because recess was a time when you played with other students, which I never did. My mom asked me if I wanted to have a friend to come home, and I said no because I did not have any friends.

"Why?" my mother asked.

"I do not go to recess so I can practice writing with my right hand because Ms. Cook said I would be stupid if I continued to write with my left hand. Moreover, Mom, I am getting pretty good at writing with my right hand. I think I can write with either hand."

"What? There is nothing wrong with writing with your left hand. I am going to the principal and Ms. Cook and stopping this assignment immediately."

Before becoming a mom, my mom taught at the school I attended, so she knew the principal and Ms. Cook personally. I do not know what was said, but I do know I was allowed to go to recess, and there were no more right-handed writing assignments. However, the damage had been done.

Yes, I could write with either hand. I was ambidextrous, but this writing process had truly messed up my ability to read, as your dominant hand and reading are directly related to each other. My second-grade teacher, Ms. Dunn, was informed about my reading problem and asked me to stay after school for a special time with her. What a deal! She would rub my back as I tried to read and give me long hugs as I improved in reading with her out loud. I remember her eyes full of encouragement, care, and, yes, love for me to read!

Yes, my first-grade teacher had traumatized me, but Ms. Dunn had loved me through this trauma: a lesson of healing trauma that I learned early. I wanted to be Ms. Dunn when I grew up, so I became a teacher of psychology. When I was teaching graduate psychology courses in northern California, one of my students said she had a friend visiting her from Georgia, where she knew I was from. He was in the student center. Would I like to meet him? Of course I would.

Well, it turned out he was from the same town as me, and his last name was Dunn. I immediately asked if he had a relative who taught second grade many years ago.

"Oh yes, my great aunt who just died last week. A very special caring lady loved by all," he said with moist eyes. We both started crying, and I could barely get my reading story out between the tears. Her presence was palpable in the student center of a graduate school in northern California some 50 years later.

*Have you had a teacher who made a difference in your life through kindness?*

*Have you ever received a message from someone deceased that you knew?*

# Bumping Heads and Hearts

In the 1990s, I attended a Buddhist retreat in Arizona, where His Holiness the Dalai Lama was supposed to help me develop a higher awareness of and compassion for humanity.

During this retreat, I, along with several other participants, stayed in a home outside of the retreat. As I was driving the rental car to the last day of the retreat, when His Holiness was supposed to give the final initiation, I hit a rock that stopped the car immediately. Other participants were in another car behind us. They stopped, and after a brief review of the situation, I insisted on waiting with the car for AAA while the others went on to the initiation. I knew I was being initiated as I waited an hour in the Arizona heat. AAA arrived as a toothless man playing deafening country-western music in his truck. He was a jovial man and quite determined to get me back to the rental dealership as soon as possible. He hauled the car and me back to the office, never slowing below 80 miles per hour.

When we arrived at the rental office, I was greeted by the rental agents with profuse apologies for renting me a low-riding car in an area they knew was not safe for such a car. It was completely their fault, my hitting the rock. "Excuse me, what are you saying?" I shockingly asked. Well, it was not only their truth, but they were now giving me a free black Cadillac to drive. I tried to say no to such a vehicle, but they insisted that was the least they could do for me.

Within minutes, I found myself driving a black Cadillac to the retreat center and pulling up into a large parking space facing a side door to the building. Immediately, the door opened, and His Holiness and entourage emerged. His Holiness came quickly toward my car, opened the back door, and sat in the back seat of my rented black Cadillac. Yes, this is true; it happened. Immediately, his translator apologized to me and told His Holiness that this was not his car, nor was I his driver. I insisted I could easily drive him wherever he needed to go, but, at that moment, the real driver with a black Cadillac pulled up behind me, and His Holiness understood the error. Or shall we say, the opportunity? As we got out of my car, we laughed and laughed. He gently put his hands on my head and pulled it toward his head. There we were, laughing and bumping our heads together. Then he pulled back, and we bowed to each other, with His

Holiness clearly saying in English, "So sorry, so sorry." I kept saying, "No problem, no problem." As he pulled away in his car, he kept waving and laughing, and I did the same.

This window of kindness transformed me. I learned that what appears to be a mistake is not, what appears to be a problem is not, what I think is going to happen is not going to happen, and what seems so serious has a depth of kindness inside of it that transforms humanity.

*Have you ever made a mistake that turned into an experience of kindness?*

*When you review your life, what circumstance stands out the most as a teacher of kindness?*

# The Quiet Student

He was quiet, mainly in the back of the room, but he always asked at the end of class if I needed any help. I sure looked like I did with all the papers and books I toted around. I was teaching an undergraduate psychology class at Sonoma State University. The students were a mix of eager and could not care less. This quiet one was keen.

His papers and questions were deep, and, of course, he earned an A. I asked him if he would be a TA for me the next term, and he accepted. We would chat after class about finding meaning in life, which was very unusual, but I soaked it up. There was a beautiful young blonde girl in the back of the class who acted like she knew nothing. He asked me after class if I thought she might be playing the role of a dumb blond.

Oh no, wait and see her papers. I bet they will be the best in the class. If you research "dumb blonde," you will find Marilyn Monroe. Who this phrase started with was not at all dumb!

Furthermore, sure enough, the blonde student handed in the best papers.

"Remember, do not be distracted by appearances. People often appear one way but are completely the opposite." I shared my little wisdom with him. He thanked me and became an outstanding person who never got distracted by appearances and dedicated his energy to those in need.

I helped him get a job caregiving for my mentor and his wife while they aged. He did not miss a beat with them and kept learning, especially from my mentor's wife, a former nun. The two had a very special understanding of giving without expecting recognition. I watched him grow from 1998 to 2022 into an unrecognized giver.

He has been to Lebanon and Ukraine five times each since the war started on funds he gathered to care for the kids during the war. He set up art places for the kids at train stations where they could draw and express their feelings about the trauma of the war. He has also gone to other countries (Libya and Jordan) to help traumatized children with art therapy. This quiet student has made a big difference to many young people in war-torn countries.

The teacher always aims to watch a student pass them, so he passed me. I am joyful for how many children and families he has touched with his kindness.

His name is Howard Dotson, and if you want more information on his work, the The link to his work is http://faithlead.org/author/howie-dotson.

*Have you expanded kindness beyond what your teachers have taught you?*

*Have you ever watched a student flourish beyond your mentorship?*

## *Laughter*

My uncle, whom we called "Bumpy" (my sister came up with this name because she could not say Uncle Gordon), would bring a Catholic priest to our Sunday family dinners at the beach house during the summers. Bumpy would bring a bottle of bourbon and tell sex jokes. My mother would regularly ask her brother to stop telling jokes because of my sister and me. The conversation would go something like this:

"Gordon, stop telling those jokes! What will the girls think?"

"They will not, but they will remember to laugh."

No one listened to Mom, and the jokes continued with the priest, my dad, me, and my sister joining in the laughter. We were not Catholic, and, to this day, I do not know why my uncle and the priest had a close friendship, but I think a big part of the friendship was based on laughing. I do not remember the content of the jokes, but the sound of the laughter I remember well. Bumpy was right, and I remember the laughter.

My son, who never knew my uncle, has my uncle's laugh. When he was about six, and we were visiting my family in Georgia, he was laughing in one room. My cousin, my uncle's daughter, asked who was laughing in the other room. She thought her father was in the next room, so she entered the room and found my son laughing.

"How can that be? He has my father's laugh!"

"Yes, I know, his laugh is very infectious. Makes you want to join, right?"

My cousin and I embraced and laughed deeply. A good laugh is so physically and emotionally healthy. Looking back over so many vast experiences in my life and others' lives, I do not know where anyone would be without a hearty laugh.

Now, my son has a son who laughs a lot. My son recently sent me a video clip of him and my grandson laughing while playing peek-a-boo. What a profound game that has passed through time and generations with so many laughs.

I know this laugh will continue, bringing much joy to my generation and beyond: a quieting realization that this goodness will outlast all losses and sorrows.

*Have you had a hearty laugh lately?*

*When has laughter had a healing effect in your life?*

# Filling Mom's Heart With Kindness

Many kindnesses emerge in the dying process, especially with the loss of a parent. Thus, it was with my 88-year-old mother. She had a heart attack and was taken to the hospital, where she had spent many hours volunteering as a pink lady. I could get there from California and be with her in her last days. As she woke up, her doctor, a person of color, was taking her pulse. She immediately asked me why the orderly was touching her.

"Mother, that is not the orderly. He is the doctor who saved your life."

"Oh no, madam, I did not save you. I am just doing my job," the doctor politely said.

"Oh yes, you did save her life," I said looking deep into his eyes. Mother looked at him and then at me with questioning eyes but no words yet.

Internally, I decided that if my mother made a fuss about

her doctor being a person of color, I would leave. However, she surprised me and thanked the doctor for saving her life. Tears rolled down my face and hers. The doctor excused himself, saying he would leave us for a private moment.

The years of arguments we had stopped. Moreover, now, she had tears of forgiveness for all those years of prejudice directed toward non-Caucasian people.

When I entered her room the next day, she asked for her lipstick, brush, and mirror, as she had said he would be there any minute.

"Who will be here?"

"Oh, come on, Myrtle, you know who I am talking about, the doctor! You know he is good-looking. Now, get my lipstick," she said as she began to primp for the doctor.

It was delightful to watch the two banter. They laughed together and made the most of every moment before she died two days later.

When the heart surgeon took over to remove water from her heart, I put my hand on her gurney and told him he had to come to get me when the surgery failed so I could talk her through her dying. He confidently said that the surgery would be successful, but I knew better. About an hour later, the head nurse came out to get me.

"Myrtle, it is Mary. I am sure you remember me from the beach."

A quick knowing hug from the beach days. She explained that the heart surgeon had said to her that the patient's California daughter had made him promise to get her if the surgery failed, which it had. Furthermore, my childhood friend came to get me as she pushed the surgeon aside, stating she knew the California daughter from playing on the Georgia beach as children. What a moment!

Mary guided me to my mother in the surgery room, where all the attendants and doctors were lined against the walls. With Mary gently rubbing my back, I leaned over Mom and gently told her she would soon be with her husband, parents, and all her dear friends. She moved slightly in my hand, and then the movement stopped. She heard me and left this earth accompanied by loving-kindness.

I went upstairs and gave her good-looking doctor a glass of carrot juice in gratitude to him for his kindness. The heart surgeon called Mary the next day, requesting to be with her while she helped patients die, as he had never been in the presence of a dying patient. The experience of my mother dying deeply moved him, and he was ready to be present for the dying process.

*Have you experienced a long prejudice dissolve before death?*

*Have you ever been present to death with kindness?*

# Am I Next for the Ultimate Kindness

There have been many endings in my life, but I have not reached my final ending, my physical death. For many years, I did hospice volunteer work as an individual and group counselor, including training others to lead bereavement groups. I learned a lot about death and bereavement during these years, but what was consistent was how very small insignificant losses in life prepare us for the significant losses of loved ones. For instance, how many earrings I have lost during my life, and with each loss the pattern was the same: relief to find it, disappointment perhaps with some sadness after never finding it, trying to match the lost earring then settling for a new pair and either tossing the only one or holding on to it in hopes one day its mate would be found. I moved on, disappointed and sad in remembering the old earring, but I move on, determined this loss would never happen again. Somehow, I will never misplace an earring again, but I will, and I do, and I move on. Over time, my longing for the lost earring diminishes and, in many cases, is forgotten. This pattern of relief, disappointment, sadness, and moving on is similar to the loss of a loved one, except with the loss of a loved one, I do not move into completely forgetting.

I always remember a dear friend I loved who was born and raised in Switzerland. More than 25 years ago, he took my husband, our son, and me on a transformative backpack trip. He guided us high into the Swiss Alps for about five days. We hiked from one hut to another, where we slept and ate warm food cooked by those who tended the huts. We had a room with bunk beds and other hikers. We were all exhausted. All that mattered was warm food and a good bed, which we had. We crossed ice fields carefully, with the help of walking sticks. He always knew where we were and where we were going. He had hiked the Swiss Alps all of his 50-plus years. I was utterly amazed at the beauty of these mountains.

Throughout my life, I have wondered about a force larger than I could see, and here I was, close to touching this wonder in the presence of these awesome Alps. I leaned into my walking sticks and looked up to see my son, almost a teenager, following in the footsteps of our dear friend, climbing higher and moving deeper into the great caldron of life, of nature. The experience inside this caldron was vast. We would stop sometimes, drink some water, and he would check if we were each physically OK. One night in a hut around a burning fire, he shared that he wanted the last day of his life to be spent hiking in the Alps. He felt certain that would happen. Moreover, for now, the Alps have transformed us into knowing for sure there is something greater than our physical body and how much care our bodies need. Sleep came easily and quickly, but his conversation stayed with me as we parted ways at the end of the trip, accompanied by hugs and thank yous for all of his kindness.

Always with a gentle smile, he would remind us that the mountains changed us. He reminded us to keep this experience close. I never saw him again but heard of his death about two years later. He was hiking with another friend in the Alps and fell to his knees. He looked up and said, "I am ready. Take me." He died immediately from a massive heart attack. His hiking friend found others to help, and he was carried out of the Alps but was returned to the Alps after his cremation. I was surprised and sad but so happy for him; his wish of how he wanted to die had transpired. This experience of the Alps with our friend and my family remains close to me. My now adult son, with his son, holds this experience close, a highlight of his growing up.

As I near my death with my aging, I am not only supported by this experience but by my near-death experience many years ago. My car was hit by another car and pushed into oncoming traffic. I hit my head against the top of the car and went unconscious. I found myself immediately in a huge, luminous green space that stretched on and on.

Suddenly, there was the presence of my mother's dear friend who had died many years ago, asking me, "What are you doing here?

"Where are we?"

She repeated her question as if to wake me up. "What are you doing here?"

I loved where I was—so peaceful, serene, and beautiful. I asked again, "Where are we?"

"What are you doing here? It is not your time."

Now, I remembered she was dead. I must be dead. I had to go back, and I did. I woke up in an emergency room in a hospital with a doctor, nurse, and police officer arguing over the fact that the police officer should not be in the emergency room. "Please, be kind to each other," I said kindly to them.

They were shocked I had returned and shocked I was instructing them to be kind. I had some stitches in my head and was dismissed to go home. However, I did not dismiss this experience, knowing that one day I would return to this incredible space I had the honor of visiting. It was not my time. I still had work to do on this planet. I was not done yet!

Stepping into one piece of my work is attending to my long, challenging relationship with my sister. We are opposites. As you might suspect from my writing, I am outspoken, and my only sibling is very proper. She lives inside a known box while I live comfortably in unknown boxes. We have lived opposite lives, both very fulfilling but very different. She lost her precious husband seven years ago to a sudden heart attack and has been challenged by integrating her loss. Recently, she was in an emergency room with sepsis UTIs, which the doctors had difficulty getting under control.

Her condition worsened, and I knew it was time to visit her. Her dear friend called me and offered to pick me up at the airport and stay with her. I humbly accepted her kind and generous offer and went to see my sister for two weeks.

She started getting better, but another diagnosis meant it was time for her to move into assisted living. Unfortunately, the journey of aging and moving into assisted living is not an uncommon experience today. Fortunately, my niece found a wonderful space for her mom.

My sister and I did what we did best: We made a joke. I

threatened to move into her spare bedroom in her assisted living apartment if she did not improve. She kept improving, as she did not want to share her space with me. Was it a joke? Yes.

Nevertheless, as jokes often do, it also pointed to the truth that neither of us wants to ever live together again. Our differences can be accepted at a distance but are undoubtedly challenging in the same space. I kept the joke alive as a form of kindness to my sister. Her kind daughter is present but stretched; I am there for her. This story is repeated many, many times in many, many families all over the world.

Will I be next in assisted living? Sure, I could, but there is the reality: I am going to die. I continue to look closely at choices around terminal illness. I have no fear of death, but dying slowly, I do fear. I search for choices vigilantly and am at ease with choosing my dying under fatal circumstances. In some parts of the world, this idea of choosing death is accepted and legal. I am searching for these possibilities for my future and openly discussing this possible choice with my son and sweetheart. This is the ultimate kindness. Yes, I have named choosing death as an ultimate kindness under fatal circumstances. Kindness is present in dying and death.

*Have you considered your dying and death?*

*Have you considered the ultimate kindness for yourself under certain circumstances?*

# Impermanence and Kindness

Being mindful helps me watch my mind rise and fall. I began to experience the impermanence of emotional states and steady myself in the reality that thoughts, emotions, and life as I know it are impermanent.

I have experienced impermanence many times with the death of friends, family, and pets.

I have learned to live side by side with different forms of death, ready to die and ready to live fully engaged with kindness. I will meet my death at some point. Preparing for this graduation on the material level is full of knowns, but how can I prepare myself for the unknowns, emotionally and spiritually? I have been part of different meditation groups during my 78 years, including Buddhist, Hindu, Methodist, Sufi, and Unity. Each has provided tremendous community support to lean into meditation and prayer for listening from the inside. The inner listening experience has kindly strengthened the reality of impermanence. Over and over in silence, I experience how emotions and thoughts change, and there is a point of steady awareness when watching this change. There are many words for this steady point. I prefer the word soul. Beyond this word is the repeated experience of a steady, quiet place observing the impermanence.

In my observation of impermanence, there is a companion to impermanence—kindness. All my losses—jobs, deaths, divorce, broken feet — are accompanied by kindness. Friends and strangers are always available to inform me; they have also been through losses. My "committee" of healers after my fall included family, friends, personal trainer (Eli, whom I regularly give the "F" word), physical therapists (Mitch and Karen), acupuncturist (Melissa, who at first came to my home with all her needles), chiropractor (Mark), naturopath (Sara), doctors, nurses, caregivers, and total strangers eager to give me kindness from naming my feet Augustus and Sparky to holding me close with laughter and tears. Their kindness healed me. Many do not know each other, yet my healing bonds them to me. I can walk now without any assistance. It is utterly amazing what kindness can do. The grace of kindness is a huge blessing in times of loss. Kindness is permanent. It is the choice of kindness we each have and the legacy of kindness we leave behind.

I continue to meet new people who have become some of the greatest teachers of my life and continue to give me more opportunities to say thank you to friends who continue to guide me in aging with dignity and grace. All of these people are active in enhancing the lives of others. They are not in the least interested in self-promotion, but what can they do to help others? Each one of them consistently offers others looks and words of kindness.

I have lived long enough to have more opportunities to say thank you and to become humble. How we each are influenced by the fact of death is unique to our nature, our bodies, and the limited and unlimited choices we make or do not make. I remember a dear friend responding humorously to death denial with, "You and Mr. Jesus are the only two I know that are not going to do it."

My death has not come yet, but it will one day. I am humbled and deeply grateful that I am still here to tell my stories to you, the reader. I am still here on this earth, working, loving, and sharing with others all the paradoxical gifts of kindness.

If you live long enough, you will tell your story of living, aging, and dying. As you age, you will enter the great mystery school where you take the keenest pleasure in holding another's hand for an hour, in laughing as you start a stream of urine, in finding it breathtaking to watch a leaf fall from a tree, or in applauding the great blue heron's return to nest in the same gnarled tree for the third, fourth, or fifth time.

If you live long enough, you will live in the moment. You may not remember people, places, events, books, yesterday, or the words you just said. You may be lost in a state of consciousness that seems miserable to some and enlightened to others. However, you will sometimes experience deep peace in what is in the moment. Moreover, choosing kindness will prevail.

"Come my friends, 'tis not too late to seek a newer world."

Alfred, Lord Tennyson, Ulysses (1833).

I invite us to live in a newer world of kindness and to forgive our past unkindness to ourselves and others. I know my unkind actions very well. They have often been my teachers.

I am fallible, as we all are. Like it or dislike it, we are connected. All the things we dislike in others are inside ourselves. A truth expanded by psychologists and theologians and lived in my life over and over.

Moreover, when my turn comes to die, I will embark on one of the greatest journeys of my life, helping those who dearly love me to remember and live the kindness I have given them. I will make difficult decisions about my body or relinquish those decisions to others.  I will hopefully be offered the newest paradigm in Western medicine by my health practitioners, which includes me and my significant others in making conscious choices about my quality of living and dying.

I invite you to join me in the possibility of a newer world led by kindness until we each embark on our final journey home.

*Did you learn a new perspective on kindness through this book?*

*Were you kind today?  Will you be kind tomorrow?*

# References

Arlen, H., & Harburg, E. Y. (1939). Somewhere over the rainbow [Song]. In *The Wizard of Oz* (Original motion picture soundtrack). MGM.

Barks, C. (Trans.). (1995). The Essential Rumi. HarperSanFrancisco.

Burns, R. (1788). Auld lang syne [Song].

Dalai Lama. (2006, October 4). Dalai Lama: Too many lives lost in Iraq. The Office of His Holiness the Dalai Lama. Holiness the Dalai Lama. https://www.dalailama.com/news/2006/dalai-lama-too-many-lives-lost-in-iraq.

Gyatso, P. & Shakya, T. (Trans.). (1998). *The autobiography of a Tibetan monk*. Snow Lion Publications.

Halliwell-Phillipps, J. O. (1886). *The nursery rhymes of England* (5th ed.). Frederick Warne & Co.

Heery, M. (2021). Looking over my shoulder. In L. Hoffman & J. Falk (Eds.), *Becoming an Existential-humanistic therapist* (pp. 116-130). University Professors Press.

Heery, M., & Richardson, G. (Eds.). (2015). *Awakening to Aging: Glimpsing the gifts of aging* (2nd ed.). Tonglen Press.

Heery, M. (1993). Hearing voices: Non-psychiatric perspective. In R. Romme & S. Escher (Eds.), *Accepting voices*. MIND Publications.

Heery, M. (1987). Inner voice experiences: An exploratory study of thirty cases. *Journal of Transpersonal Psychology, 21*(1), 73-82.

Laméris, D. (2019, September 19). Small kindness. *The New York Times*.

Mother Teresa. (1995). *A simple path*. Ballantine Books.

Oliver, M. (2016). *Blue Horses*. Penguin Books.

Rogers, R., & Evans, D. (1952). Happy trails [Song].

Tennyson, A. L. (1974). *The poetical works of Tennyson*. Houghton Mifflin.

Vacha, R. (2019). *The heart of tracking*. Mount Vision Press.

# Acknowledgements

It takes a village to write and publish a book. I give immense gratitude to my village for making my memoir a reality. First, my dear friend, editor, designer, and organizer, Susan Gumucio, visited me frequently in rehab and birthed the idea of my memoir. Instead of reading so many books, she encouraged me to start my memoir. Thank you, Susan. More support for my writing came from my dear partner Phil, my immediate family (Jamie, Michelle, Dalton), friends, colleagues, and students. I am deeply grateful to each of you.

A big thank you to my many readers, editors, and organizers: Donna Benedetti, Emily Fitleberg, Lakota Lynn Grace, Michelle Horan, Ashli Landaverde, Tony Marano, Cornelia Pinnell, Sue Turner, Zoe Kriegler-Wenk, Terry Vitorelo, and Dana Vitorelo. In addition, Will Rogers, with faithful legal guidance. Everyone contributed needed suggestions with kindness extraordinaire!

Furthermore, I thank Bailey Olsen, my book designer, who painted and designed the cover, back, and inside! Thank you from California to Illinois!

Big Kindness to all of you!

# *Epilogue*

### Never Too Late To Dance

Myrtle, age 78, Belize

www.ingramcontent.com/pod-product-compliance
Lightning Source LLC
Chambersburg PA
CBHW051939290426
44110CB00015B/2037